the

AGONY

and the

AGONY

ALSO BY BETTY LONDERGAN

I'm Too *Sexy* for My Volvo

the AGONY *and the* AGONY

Raising Your Teenager without Losing Your Mind

BETTY LONDERGAN

Da Capo
∞
LIFE
LONG

A Member of
the Perseus Books Group

Many of the designations used by manufacturers and sellers to distinguish
their products are claimed as trademarks. Where those designations appear
in this book and Da Capo Press was aware of a trademark claim, the designations
have been printed in initial capital letters.

Copyright © 2008 by Betty Londergan

Designed by Linda Harper
Set in 11 point Berkeley by the Perseus Books Group

Cataloging-in-Publication data for this book is available from the
Library of Congress.

First Da Capo Press edition 2008
ISBN: 978-1-60094-074-3

Published by Da Capo Press
A Member of the Perseus Books Group
www.dacapopress.com

Note: The information in this book is true and complete to the best of our
knowledge. This book is intended only as an informative guide for those
wishing to know more about health issues. In no way is this book intended to
replace, countermand, or conflict with the advice given to you by your own
physician. The ultimate decision concerning care should be made between you
and your doctor. We strongly recommend you follow his or her advice.
Information in this book is general and is offered with no guarantees on the
part of the author or Da Capo Press. The author and publisher disclaim all
liability in connection with the use of this book. The names and identifying
details of people associated with events described in this book have been
changed. Any similarity to actual persons is coincidental.

Da Capo Press books are available at special discounts for bulk purchases in the
U.S. by corporations, institutions, and other organizations. For more information,
please contact the Special Markets Department at the Perseus Books Group, 2300
Chestnut Street, Suite 200, Philadelphia, PA, 19103, or call (800) 810-4145,
extension 5000, or e-mail special.markets@perseusbooks.com.

10 9 8 7 6 5 4 3 2

"I would there were no age between

ten and three-and-twenty,

or that youth would sleep out the rest;

for there is nothing in the between

but getting wenches with child,

wronging the anciently,

stealing, fighting."

William Shakespeare

This book is dedicated to Lulu—
my inspiration, infuriation
and infinite delight.

CONTENTS

Introduction
Welcome to Agony

I REMEMBER THE DAY IT HAPPENED.

I woke up, sunshine was streaming through the windows, and I strolled happily into my 11-year-old daughter's room to get her up for school. Raising the window shade, I chirped, "Rise and shine, sweetie! It's a bright, sunny day!"

Lulu never lifted her head from the pillow. From under the covers, she snarled, "Would you stop coming in every stupid morning and opening my blinds! Just leave me alone and stop touching my stuff!"

"Well, somebody woke up on the wrong side of the bed," I replied, leaning down to kiss her sweet cheek.

"Get off me!" she screeched, as if I'd set her limbs on fire. "And get *out of my room!*"

Stunned, I stumbled back out of Lulu's room, and went down the hall to awaken my 11-year-old stepson. In the gloom of his abode, I could barely make out his silhouette, fully clad in the gigantic sweatpants and sweatshirt that he'd worn to school the day before. He was even wearing his clod-hopper boots—on the nice clean duvet!

"Tyler! It's time to get up, honey," I said. "And you really shouldn't wear your clothes to bed. It's unsanitary."

Turning his head, he gave me a hate-filled glare, no doubt fueled by my unwise choice of the word "sanitary," which in the male adolescent lexicon can only be attached to the equally excruciating "napkin." He rolled over, pulled his blanket over his head, and grunted. *"Getouttamyroom."*

And so it begins.

❧

You go to sleep feeling blessed and secure in the loving bosom of your family, and you wake up to find your daughter is possessed. Your son has turned into some kind of zombie. And there is nothing that you can do about it, short of living through the next five or six years with this . . . creature.

How could this happen to you? To your divorced sister or to those slackers across the street who never edge their lawn or recycle—yeah, you'd expect their kids to turn out like this. But *your* kids? They're gifted, for chrissakes. They're Scouts!

Adolescence, I've learned, comes as a brutal shock to every parent. One day your child is waving goodbye to you on the school bus until he can't see you anymore, and the next, he's flipping you the finger as he slams his way out the door. The parental fall from adoration to agony happens so fast and seemingly irrevocably, it feels like somebody sucker-punching you in the gut. Every morning.

It's heartbreaking to see the face in which you once took such delight—in which you see yourself and all your best hopes—looking back at you with pure loathing. It's equally terrifying to have to sit back and witness your precious child making boneheaded choices that will make his life infinitely more difficult. My friend Teresa became so despondent when her 16-year-old son started doing drugs and flunking school that she didn't call me, or any of her friends, for three *years*. For a thousand days, she stayed in her house, worked, and tried not to go crazy.

The pain of dealing with your defiant, screwed-up teen is matched only by the shame you feel both for your child's terrible behavior and for the obviously inept parenting that produced it. Sometimes it's hard to say who's more depressed in your household, you or your hormone-flooded adolescent.

No, there is nothing funny about raising a teenager.

Which is precisely why I believe it's time for a book that *is*.

c✦Ɔ

From the moment your precious little angel starts channeling Lil' Kim to the hour your young lad stomps off to college in his big, stupid ghetto pants, *The Agony and the Agony* is there for you. This is the book to keep by your bedside as you're crying yourself to sleep after another teen tirade of "I can't believe you didn't get me a new can of hairspray today *when I specifically asked you to!* You have ruined my life and I *hate everything* about you!"

You may also want to keep a second copy in the kitchen. It'll come in handy when you're clenching your teeth as your teen food critic rants, "I cannot *believe* you made teriyaki chicken again! Is that the only freaking thing you know how to cook?"

In fact, you may even want to pack an emergency copy in the car for the inevitable onslaught of backseat driving: "Why did you turn here when you *know* this is the slowest possible way to go? You are *such a jerk!*"

In so many ways, on so many days, *The Agony and the Agony* will commiserate and accompany you on the long, lonely road of adolescence.

If you're the parent of a teen, chances are you're already sobbing your eyes out on a daily basis, or you would be if you had a lick of understanding of what's going on around you. But for some mysterious reason, we parents lock ourselves away with our doubts and self-recrimination at the very time we need somebody to second that emotion. God knows your kids are out there on YouTube and Facebook getting 24/7 tech support for the nightmare of having to live with you.

So, where's *your* peer support?

Welcome to the Whine Room—for parents only. *The Agony and the Agony* deals with the joys of raising a teen in today's permissive, promiscuous, overscheduled, underhanded, rap-infested, SAT-obsessed, value-deprived, high-anxiety culture. It will explain the phenomenon whereby puberty and menopause occur simultaneously in a family, thus creating the perfect storm of emotional chaos. It will clarify that when your teen seems to hate you, she actually *does* hate you—but it's supposed to be that way. It will quietly take your hand and walk you through the five stages of grief as you cope with losing your beloved child and inheriting the quasi-adult formerly known as your baby.

Yes, as the teen years come upon you with all the stealth and subtlety of a mortar attack, you may be tempted to ask yourself, "Where did I go wrong? How did I bring this horror upon myself?"

I say that these are the wrong questions to ask.

"Where can I go for a long, long time? And who can I blame?" are far healthier, more rational responses.

The pain of separating and the undeniable need for it are precisely what make adolescence such a challenge both for parents (feeling the pain) and for teens (feeling the undeniable need). To my mind, the journey uncannily resembles the process of coping with a death (i.e., the loss of your cute little child). So I've borrowed the five stages of grief from Elizabeth Kübler-Ross to explain the odyssey. Chapters have been divided into stages that correspond roughly to a progression through the teen years:

STAGE 1: DENIAL
      (Ages 12–13, The PreHysteric Era)
STAGE 2: ANGER
      (Ages 14–15, The Feudal Age)
STAGE 3: DEPRESSION
      (Ages 12–18, The Hellacious Period)
STAGE 4: BARGAINING
      (Ages 16–17, The Seismic Era)
STAGE 5: ACCEPTANCE
      (Age 18, The Gladit'sover Epoch)

Mathematically inclined parents may note that depression has the longest reign and acceptance is abbreviated, but don't panic. The whole process is anything but linear; these are only estimates. You may never move beyond Denial, or you may prove to be a parent/savant and bounce directly into Acceptance (in which case, you ought to write your own damn book). The important things to remember are the immortal words of King Solomon: *This too shall pass.* And the immortal words of mine: *Please pass the wine.*

Herewith, a brief description of the five stages of parenting a teen.

STAGE 1: DENIAL

Parental Symptoms: You refuse to acknowledge that your child is growing up and try desperately to ignore the signs that adolescence is in the house.

Stage Characteristics: Most people will attempt to avoid making decisions or taking action at this point.

There are none so blind as those who will not see. Luckily, teenagers will do much of the enlightenment work for you by wrecking your car, getting pregnant, or flunking out of school. Or at the very least, they'll develop zits, boobs, and a filthy mouth—all signs that you need to stop thinking of them as toddlers and realize that this big horrible person swaggering in front of you is actually your darling child, half grown-up. You're going to have to start doing a few things differently.

STAGE 2: ANGER

Parental Symptoms: You exhibit a veritable kitchen sampler of emotions: steaming, stewing, hissing, frothing, and boiling (but hopefully not whipping anything besides yourself into a frenzy).

Stage Characteristics: Most of one's energy is directed at emotional interactions rather than at problem-solving.

Yes, it is difficult to "problem-solve" during this stage because:

a. you've grounded the kid . . . for life—not for the weekend, not for the month, but for the *rest of his natural-born life* and you are not kidding this time; or

b. you've locked yourself in your bathroom so you can't physically harm anyone, or simply because that's where you've stashed the emergency flask; or
c. you're willing to consider only solutions that include a tearful parent/teen appearance on *Dr. Phil*, followed swiftly by boot camp or military school.

STAGE 3: DEPRESSION

Parental Symptoms: Everything seems pointless, overwhelming, and joyless and you can no longer remember a single nice thing about anybody in your so-called family.

Stage Characteristics: Many find it hard to cope with the demands of daily life. Ask for help from a family member, friend, or professional if needed.

Whatever you do, do not ask for your teenager's help. At this point, petitioning her to do so much as change the toilet paper roll will inevitably bring down another firestorm of teen outrage, as in: "Why do I have to do it? It's gross! And I can't believe you used the words 'toilet paper'—that is disgusting!" This exchange will doubtlessly plunge you into a deeper, more long-lasting depression than the one you're already in.

STAGE 4: BARGAINING

Parental Symptoms: You begin to have thoughts that don't begin with "Why is this happening to me?" You're empowered to take action and (metaphorically) kick some teen butt.

Stage Characteristics: People are able to express their feelings and become open to exploring options and alternatives.

Things are looking up! Instead of avoiding all contact with the outside world because your kid is such an utter annoyance, you begin to think outside the box. You explore all kinds of alternatives. For instance: Why *not* send her on a five-year expedition with Outward Bound? (They don't even use toilet paper!) Or you end a chronic source of conflict with this snappy retort: "If you refuse to take out the trash again, young man, I'm going to dump it all in your backpack." Creativity flourishes!

STAGE 5: ACCEPTANCE

Parental Symptoms: You begin to entertain the joyous possibility that your teen will not end up living in a dumpster and you will again have a life free of morning tirades, evening hysterics, and a blizzard of detention notices in the mail.

Stage Characteristics: People begin to accept the loss and look for new purpose and meaning in their lives.

This stage generally begins about thirty minutes after you drop the kid off at college and is marked by profound sadness, followed immediately by a blinding stab of ecstasy. Your kid is now his or her own responsibility. At the very least, you no longer have to sit around and witness his lunacy on a daily basis. Decision-making and problem-solving become a snap! "Hell yeah, let's buy that Mini Cooper that'll be crushed like a Coke can upon impact!" and "Weekend trip to Vegas? Count me in!" You'll feel decades younger—at least until Thanksgiving or when the first semester's grades appear.

⇝

Finally, *The Agony and the Agony* is sprinkled with stories from other parents in the form of Agonizing Examples and Words of Wisdom. I've also included Tales from Post-Teens, the recounting of young adults who look back on their recent teen years and explain why they did those infuriating things. What it all meant. And how they're making their lives a success now that their frontal lobes are hard as granite and they can finally think clearly.

Courage, parental units! It could happen.

For now, agony awaits.

Stage 1: Denial

AGES 12–13,
THE PREHYSTERIC ERA

IT'S A CRYING SHAME KIDS HAVE TO GROW UP. THEY arrive in a fanfare of drama, almost ripping you stem to stern in the process, then proceed to develop into darling, heart-stealing little characters. They lisp, say adorable things, look at you with gigantic saucer eyes—and they really, really like you. Not to be too Sally Fields here, but that is a fairly irresistible, ego-gratifying trait. Your children want to look like you. They want to walk and talk like you. Most of all, they want to please you and make you happy.

And so, you make the fatal mistake of assuming that your little girl will spend the rest of her days singing little songs that end with "We're a happy fam-i-ly!" Or that your young son will always wait breathlessly for Father's Day so he can wake you by jumping on your bed with a platter of soggy pancakes and a nosegay of wilted carnations. You live in this fool's paradise for about eleven years and then adolescence descends upon you like a plague. You feel cheated and betrayed—but mostly stunned—at this unforeseen turn of events.

Childhood won't last.

It can't last.

Why? Why???

Well, for starters, what parent with two shreds of aortic material would ever let a kid like that saunter out of his life? You'd have to be crazy to let that cherub go! Ergo, in nature's mysterious, indifferent march of progress, those babies we love disappear. Like frost on a late-September morning. Like the streaks of apricot in an evening sky. Like the last delicious sip of the icy martini in which you're attempting to drown your parental sorrows.

Poof! Gone.

Yet the shock and awe remain. Even if you logically understood that this growing-up thing was bound to happen, the reality may hit you like a torrent of cold, wet grief. You'll stand by helplessly as your glorious lad morphs into a sullen, perspiring doofus whose one intelligible word is "yuh." You'll watch in dismay as your lovely girl chews her way out of childhood's cocoon and emerges a mouthy, hysterical teen.

The first stage of this huge transformation may be a wee bit hard to accept, as it represents a process of estrangement from the person you love most in the world. The word "estrangement" comes from the French word *etranger*, or stranger, which is what your child may become to you. It also sounds a lot like the good old English word "strange," which is a polite, understated way to describe your new teen. He will pierce some body parts and begin to resemble Boy George. She will slather on mascara like Tammy Faye Bakker and do frightening things to her eyebrows. Strange strangers, these people formerly known as your children.

Faced with that uncomfortable reality, some parents will slip into denial. Personally, I feel that denial has gotten a very bad rap and is, in fact, a superb coping mechanism. So deny away. It's okay. We both realize it won't stop your child's awful aging process, but it may get you through to the next stage when you can get ferociously angry about it. Now that's something to live for!

Until then, let's wander through a few of the signs and symptoms that your baby's done gone.

1

FIRST SIGNS OF
ADOLESCENCE AND
OTHER HORRORS

THE FIRST SIGNS OF IMPENDING ADOLESCENCE ARE usually verbal (as in: "You're not the boss of me!"). Yet most painful are the physical signs that offer irrefutable proof your kid is growing up. The first time you see a pubic hair, for instance, your child is still likely to be young enough to take a bath and okay with your seeing his or her naked body. Sneak a discreet peek, for you are likely never to see that adorable innocent skin again. Seemingly overnight, the flesh that came from you, that you knit in your very womb or called into being with your seed, will be snatched away and claimed exclusively by its rightful owner.

ARE THOSE BREASTS??

At first, it may seem as if you will be invited along on this developmental journey, as your child wonders at the incredible bodily changes taking place. She'll walk into your bedroom while you're busy trying to find the missing mate to thirty-eight abandoned socks, raise her arm, and display a tiny thicket of brown tucked into a formerly smooth armpit. Or he'll amble in and introduce you to the shadowy whisper of fuzz sprouting on his darling upper lip. You will gag to yourself (while making sure that your face maintains the look of reverent fascination you reserve for Jacques Cousteau specials) and exclaim, "Wow, this means you're becoming a young lady/young man! I am so proud of you!"

Then you'll stomp into the closet where your spouse is methodically tossing out mismatched socks and holler, "What the hell have you been feeding that kid to bring on the early onset of puberty? I told you to lay off the goddamned soy!"

Your beloved partner will look at you with pity and remark that the kid is 12. This is natural. And by the way, O You of Limited Awareness, the kid hasn't touched anything with soy in it for years.

Hair is merely the first hurdle in the triathlon of adolescence. You will also notice an alarming increase in the overall amount of flesh, particularly in the chest and shoulder area of girls. These are called breasts and/or boobs and, yes, your daughter will get them whether you think she should or not. She's likely to be, in equal parts, proud and mortified about these new appendages. The route of least psychological damage is to pretend to notice nothing specific—denial at work here!—and remain neutrally in favor of breasts as a concept. (Example: *"They're good no matter what size they are and yours look fine to me; now please make your bed."*)

AGONIZING EXAMPLE

Jack owns an advertising agency and is very creative. Sometimes that creativity spills over into his home life. By the time his daughter Sydney turned 13, her breasts were fully developed, so Jack and his younger son made up a funny song about them set to the tune of "What's New, Pussycat?" Whenever the over-endowed lass came to the dinner table, father and son would launch into the chorus, belting out, "What's that in your shirt? Whoa, whoa, whoo-ooa!" to serenade her arrival. A couple months later, Sydney took up ice hockey, a sport that involves full-body coverage, quilted padding, and chest protectors—all of which she probably wore to *class*, given her father's wildly inappropriate sense of humor.

Boys simply swell up, horizontally and/or vertically. This will result in fleeting feelings of superiority, self-loathing, and excruciating self-consciousness. At which point, boys will generally remove themselves from public display and disappear into their rooms, there to remain for the duration of adolescence. Unlike girls who crave attention and hysteria—no matter how negative or pointless—boys simply cannot handle the onslaught of emotions and will flee to the dark, silent peace of their private space.

Of course, they're also in there pleasuring themselves to the point of passing out—but that's another chapter.

Your child's skin is also likely to erupt in a fireworks display of excess hormones, a scourge of adolescence many of us painfully remember. Acne is the final insult to a teen already convinced that his or her life is a wreckage too extreme to salvage, so it's

TALES FROM POST-TEENS • • • • • • • •

My mom had a holistic, homeopathic approach to skin care. She kept wanting me to put raw egg white, oil of geranium, and all this other natural crap on my face, but all I wanted was a little Proactiv like I saw on TV. I begged and begged for it, but she was convinced it was a carcinogen and would end up being terribly bad for me. I suffered through all those years with awful skin, being desperately self-conscious. I'm still bitter at her for not doing more to help me. My advice is that sometimes it's important to go mainstream even if it's not something you believe in personally. It may not work out any better than your creative methods, but at least your teen will know you're trying to help and you won't have to take the (total) blame later.

highly recommended that you do whatever you can to help your teen cope with skin problems, no matter how deeply in denial you are. Dermatologists, prescriptions, and endless tubes of Clean & Clear: Yes, it's going to cost a fortune but if you can afford it, it's probably worth at least trying to throw a rope to your teen. (Although in truth, the best and certainly cheapest thing your child can do is wash his face often and keep his mitts off the blemishes. And by the way, always remember to call them "blemishes." It sounds more civil and less disfiguring than "zits" or the dreaded "pimples.")

Teens won't thank you for your skin intervention. In fact, they're likely to blame you for the defective acne gene you passed along to them, *"probably on purpose!!"* But in the years to come, they will remember you tried to help.

All these physical changes of adolescence are meant to help you, the denier, see that your child is growing into an adult, and act as an inescapable roadmap of what is to come. Look beyond the changes you desperately wish weren't happening and try to marvel at them. At the very least, pretend to enthusiastically embrace and admire the hairy, breasty, blemish-ridden person who has taken the place of your cute baby.

HAVING "THE TALK"

In an ABC News survey of adults, 90 percent of parents said they talked with their teenagers about sex, but a survey of teens revealed only 49 percent of teens say they did. Clearly, whatever the parents thought was a conversation about sex, the kids didn't hear it that way.

—ABC News Poll:
"Sex Lives of American Teens" (May 19, 2006)

Well, excuse *me*. As somebody who has "conversations" with teens all the time, I can tell you that they have highly selective hearing. Somebody's fibbing here, and my money's on the 41 percent of teens whose parents *did* talk to them, and probably *did* impart some very important, sensitive, and enlightening information—yet were not heard. Maybe it didn't register as a conversation because the teens involved didn't hear what they wanted and so, the discussion "never happened." That's what my research reveals on a daily basis.

Everybody tells you how important it is to have "The Talk" with your child when he or she approaches puberty. Moms agonize over the responsibility of their daughters' sexual education, practice frank and pithy speeches in front of

AGONIZING EXAMPLE

Candy hates her daughter's school dances. The last time she picked up Ashley from a seventh-grade dance, her daughter was very upset. Being a nosy mom, Candy was dying to find out what had happened, but she'd learned not to interrogate. Eventually Ashley blurted out, "Julie is so annoying!"

Candy thinks Ashley's friend Julie is frighteningly sophisticated and sort of slutty, but she played it low-key and said, "Well, what did Julie do?"

"I was standing there with Jordan," Ashley explained, "and she started going on about how I'm still a virgin and why didn't Jordan take care of that. She just wouldn't shut up!"

Candy almost started hyperventilating and was dying to race back and give Julie a good talking-to, but she merely muttered something innocuous like "Well, it doesn't sound like Julie acted like a very good friend."

Ashley whipped around and screamed, "Mom, Julie is my best friend! You are such a jerk! This is why I never tell you anything!!!"

So much for the low-key approach.

TALES FROM POST-TEENS ● ● ● ● ● ● ● ●

My mom's advice on sex was pretty lame. Basically, I remember two things that she thought would guide me safely through my teen years: (1) "You are not allowed to jump on the trampoline with boys; they'll just try to bump into you and touch your boobs." And (2) "Well . . . it wasn't exactly penetration." (This was my mom's response when I asked her if she'd had premarital sex, after she asked me if I was having sex with one of my high school boyfriends.) You can't lie to your teenager, especially about sex. They'll immediately know you're lying, and then blow off anything you're trying to tell them.

the mirror, and whip up anxiety the size of a tornado. Dads generally take a more low-key approach with their sons. In fact, that approach can sometimes dip extremely low: One guy I know streamlined the process by taking his 13-year-old son to a strip joint, firing up a cigar, and asking, "Any questions?"

I tried to have "The Talk" with Lulu, but every time I'd clear my throat and launch into my prepared speech, she'd stammer in panic, "Mom, I know all this stuff, okay? I know about it, so stop talking!!!" and flee from the room. I attempted to have "The Talk" in the car to cut off her exit strategy, until I realized she was fully prepared to hurl herself from a moving vehicle rather than suffer through my sex education lecture. Finally in desperation, I bought the coolest-looking book I could find that promised to cover "Everything you need to know about sex, boys, your body, etc." and tossed it on her bed. I felt marginally relieved when I noticed it was being read and then stuffed under her bed. However, when I read in the *New York Times* about the prevalence of oral sex in middle school (and this was confirmed in a harrowing discussion with the school guidance counselor), I decided I couldn't afford to be so passive. Clearly, my lecture on oral issues wasn't going to happen orally unless I was prepared for Lulu to spend the next few months in a body cast. Instead, I wrote a few long letters explicitly telling her what I wanted her to know about sex. Much to my amazement she read those letters and kept them. I still feel disappointed that we couldn't personally speak on the subject, but what I cared most about—articulating my thoughts and values about how precious her heart, mind and body are—I believe I did communicate. This was "The Talk" I most needed to have, even if it was on paper.

Why Do You Think They Call Them AdoleSCENTS?

Thanks to the soup of hormones that is now simmering in your adolescent's body, you're heading into an avalanche of olfactory changes. Your baby doesn't smell like the same person you gave birth to and, to be blunt, the change is not for the better.

The first chink in the chain occurs when you lean down to kiss your precious child good morning and you're hit with a sour odor that seems weirdly familiar—surely she inherited that morning breath directly from your husband!

You chuck out her natural toothpaste from Vermont and switch to Flavor Crystal Extreme Freshening Turbo Gel, then take pains not to put your face anywhere near hers until she's brushed first.

The next nasal assault takes place when you're driving your son home from his soccer match. He takes off his shoes and the smell almost knocks you out of your seat. Naturally, you assume you've driven by an oil refinery or sulfur plant; that odor couldn't possibly be your sweet child! You quickly roll up the windows, thereby sealing in the aromas that have already intensified. "Honey, are those your . . . socks I'm smelling?" you ask gently.

"Mom, I can't help it if you never wash them!" he answers testily and completely inaccurately. "Besides, my feet sweat in these shoes!"

You immediately bang a U-turn, swerve into the next mall you see, and buy $75 new cleats. The next day, they smell every bit as bad as the old pair. You start driving with all the car windows open, even in five-degree weather. And instead of burying your nose in the beloved clothes of your child, you now hold all his dirty laundry items at an arm's length.

The last, most undeniable domino to topple is your child's cute bedroom, which will descend from smelling of talcum powder and lavender into the funk of a middle school boys' locker room. Lest you mistakenly assume that boys smell worse than girls, be forewarned. It isn't necessarily so. Boys tend to be compulsive shower-takers, possibly due to the opportunity for self-pleasuring that locked bathroom doors offer, and that compulsive showering tends to ameliorate the reek. Girls have all the complicated scents of womanhood to deal with and trust me, not everything comes up smelling like roses.

Keeping odors down in a house full of teen spirit is a work in progress. And you're about to develop a nose for it. Encourage (i.e., enforce) daily showers and good personal hygiene, and start buying deodorant (not antiperspirant) for your teens by age 12, at the latest. Teach them how to do laundry and employ the "sniff test" on their own clothes.

WORDS OF WISDOM

Kate is a closet smoker. In an extreme effort to cover her tracks and model good, healthy behavior for her kids, she's become a Febreze addict. She lights up in the basement, puffs her brains out, and then sprays every inch of her body to prevent detection by her family, who all know perfectly well that she's down there smoking.

Over the years, Kate has become convinced that she's going to die, not of lung cancer but of Febreze poisoning. She might be right. If you've developed a similarly unhealthy dependence on artificial room fresheners or those awful plug-ins, open your windows (this is not a metaphor), switch to a natural citrus product, and stop poisoning yourself and your stinky kids.

Then stockpile scented candles for when you desperately need to blot out all scents of them.

IT'S 11 A.M.
DO YOU KNOW WHERE YOUR TEENAGER IS?

This is so obvious, you'd have to be in serious denial not to know the answer. Which is *in bed*, of course. Sleeping. Snoozing. Snoring. Dead to the world and decidedly not to be resurrected anytime soon.

Yes, thanks to the Boomer fixation on providing our offspring with all the amenities of hotel living right in their very own homes, our teens have developed an unhealthy addiction to the phrase "Do Not Disturb." Last time I checked, we parents were not getting paid to offer breakfast at 2 P.M. or facilitate room service. I refuse to tiptoe around this issue, even though I, too, have failed to administer the wake-up call.

Yes, after years of berating my husband for allowing his kids to wallow in bed until noon on weekends, I caved like the hypocrite I am and now allow my daughter to remain in a state of unconsciousness for hours on Saturday mornings. Basically, I'm hoping to repay some of the sleep debt she's acquired by staying up late doing homework and text-messaging the planet on school nights, then rising at 6 A.M. to straighten her already stick-straight hair before leaving for the train at 7:05 in a whirlwind of missing socks and bitter accusations that I'm ruining her life by making her eat breakfast. Like every other weary parent of a teen, I've compromised my principles in an utterly futile attempt to please my daughter with these indulgent sleep-a-thons. In return, she will snarl at me with venom when I've awoken her at 11:30 A.M., berating me for not letting her "sleep in."

"Sleep in?" I ask, bewildered. "Into what? Monday?"

At the onset of adolescence, you have one fleeting chance to derail this slacker sleep pattern. It *is* possible. Oh sure, I've read all the research studies saying that shifting teenage metabolisms force kids to stay awake late into the night, and that their circadian rhythms simply will not allow them to go to sleep until after they've watched *Jay Leno*, *The Daily Show*, and *Growing Up Gotti*. However, I think it's far more likely that teens aren't physically tired enough to fall asleep because, all day long, they haven't exercised anything other than their text-messaging/video-playing thumbs.

Do you think our parents would have wasted five minutes worrying about whether we were "ready" to go to sleep? Or if we were planning to "sleep in" instead of getting up to do chores on Saturday? They said lights out, came in and physically turned the lights out, and we quickly became too bored, lying there in the dark hating them, to do anything but nod off. And they didn't tiptoe around on Saturday mornings trying to protect our slumber, either.

In my heart, I adamantly believe sleep must be taken more seriously. Or more appropriately, I believe we parents need to enforce the bedtime rule. If teens go to bed at a decent hour, they will be able to drag their butts out of bed before noon, and you can bet they're not doing anything productive in the wee hours of the night anyhow. Unfortunately, after a week of work, parents are far more likely to be passed out on the sofa by 10:30 P.M. and thus physically incapable of staying up to enforce bedtime. It's an exhausting quandary, complicated by the fact that we want to be liked by our kids—an impossible dream our parents didn't waste one ounce of energy striving to achieve.

To be a tad gentler, however, I'll admit that most kids are crazily overscheduled during the week and the weekend is the only time they can relax. Like a pack of mad gerbils on a treadmill, they desperately need the downtime so they can continue the race to nowhere—I mean, to the Ivy Leagues, the NBA, and all the other places we're pushing them to go.

My half-assed compromise is that I usually let Lulu sleep in on Saturday mornings, then make her get up at 9:00 on Sundays to go to church. It's not a perfect system but at least I feel like I haven't totally given up the cause for consciousness. If you can get your child involved in something he or she wants to do weekend mornings, perhaps you won't have to fight the battle of rising.

Ultimately, if you, like me, are driven crazy by your kids' sleeping habits but do acquiesce to their appeals to snooze, there is a saving grace. Completely on his own, your teenager

TALES FROM POST-TEENS ● ● ● ● ● ● ● ● ●

I don't remember being that lazy as a teen, but while look-ing at photos of myself during my high school days I noticed that in every single one of them I was lying on the sofa. I don't think my mom has a single vertical photo of me from that time.

will likely come to regret stumbling downstairs at 2 P.M., hav-ing wasted the entire day. Or so I dream.

SLOTH AND FULL-BODY LETHARGY

When I went to Costa Rica, I had the opportunity to witness a real live sloth in "action." Twenty of us clustered around the base of a tree, looking up at the shaggy animal hanging by his arms above us. About two hours into our sloth-watch, I jerked awake and realized I was not in a coma. The animal *had* moved approximately three inches along the branch, with another foot to go before reaching its scintillating desti-nation of another branch. The upside of sloth-watching is that it prepares you for a lifetime of watching CSPAN, as it makes Joseph Lieberman look like Mick Jagger by compari-son. The downside, at least for a Type A personality like my-self, is that it can bring out feelings of aggressiveness and extreme frustration. I wanted to zap the inane animal with a taser for at least the illusion of motion.

Remind you of anybody *you* know?

Yes, teenagers do take slothfulness to a whole new level, although sadly that's the only thing they will move upward—unlike their clothes, their shoes, or their algebra grades. It's maddening and disappointing, particularly for parents of previously zippy, sparky young kids, to watch them hit the teen years.

And slow down . . .

To the point of . . .

Undetectable . . .

Motion.

My Lulu used to swing for hours outside, pumping her little legs in a furious effort to go higher and higher, and hang by her arms for so long I thought her little shoulders were going to pop out of joint. Now, to see her climb a flight of stairs is to know exactly what she's going to look like at 90, as the stupendous effort it takes to put a foot on one riser after another is apparently exhausting every available resource in her body.

My stepkids have likewise convinced many worried adults that they are suffering from chronic fatigue syndrome. In their orbit, no sofa is safe from sprawl and they are equal-opportunity floppers. Whether it's an Italian silk chaise or a smoke-infused flea-market remnant, they will plop down and remain motionless and content for hours. Even without a plasma flat-screen in front of them. While this at first struck me with great dismay, I now feel confident the kids have a secure future as models in a life-drawing class. And at least we can be sure they're not suffering from hyperactivity disorder.

Slothful habits go hand-in-glove with the elongated sleeping patterns described earlier, until your house may begin to resemble the Land of the Living Dead. Perhaps it's the deluge of hormones that is rendering teens chemically inert. Or maybe it's those big, stupid clothes they wear, which actually

Agonizing Example

In high school, Margaret's son Charles was totally over-scheduled with Advanced Placement courses, music, student government, and varsity sports. He got home every day about 7 or 8 P.M., did four hours of homework, then collapsed. Margaret didn't work and Charles was her only child, so she never wanted to ask him to help around the house. She washed, folded, and put away Charles's laundry from the day he was born. She made his bed, changed his sheets, ironed his clothes, and brought meals to his room to allow him to study while he ate. When Charles finally went off to college, he was untouched by a single domestic skill. The first week, he had to ask his Dorm Resident, Kip, who'd grown up in a military family, how to use a washing machine and iron. Kip called a meeting of everybody on the floor to explain to Charles and all the other "spoiled rotten brats" these basic chores. Naturally, Charles immediately called his mother and demanded to know why the hell he hadn't been taught anything he really needed to know in life.

prevent movement. All I know is this: Your teen is likely entering a state of extended torpor. The only things you can do are avert your gaze and get used to it, or give them some chores to pry them off the sofa.

You know your kids aren't too busy to do a little work around the house; you simply don't have the backbone to make them do it. Me neither. Some folks suggest you create a "chore chart"—sweep the floors, clean a bathroom, rake the yard, and so on—and then tie the task to their allowance or going out. I can't quite get behind the chart concept because it reminds me of camp. Instead, I make charts for *myself* and pretend I've shared them with Lulu. If I can get her to do something, I check the task off triumphantly but *no way* is it something that works to motivate her. Of course, it is your responsibility to teach your kid some basic life skills and at the very least, giving them chores will save you from totally enabling their sloth.

Then you can reclaim the TV and tune in to CSPAN to catch some real action.

Whose Body Is It, Anyway?

From piercings to hair dye, the beginnings of adolescence bring up all kinds of interesting questions, but this one is particularly flummoxing. In your heart, you know the correct answer: Your child's body belongs to him or her. Perhaps, like my stepson Tyler, he'll stake his claim by shoving a needle through his earlobe at age 12, and you'll get that cheerful call from the guidance counselor that he's bleeding all over his math homework. Or your daughter will shave her eyebrows off in do-it-yourself cosmetic surgery. With great reluctance, you will be forced to confront the reality that you're not going to be able to maintain autocratic control of your fiefdom forever.

And yet, you've got a lot invested in that little package. You built it; you have tremendous familiarity and a ferocious desire to protect every nook and cranny of it. Your child, however, couldn't give a rat's ass about your proprietary rights and stridently demands that you immediately turn over sole authority to him. Even as you struggle to hold on, you need to realize the inevitability of your child's independence and keep it in mind as a long-term goal. Eventually, you *will* end up turning over the keys to the kingdom, but it's wise to make a slow withdrawal from the territory so your teen doesn't totally screw up the healthy infrastructure you have worked so hard to create.

WORDS OF WISDOM

I could write the chapter on this one (wait, I already did!), as way down deep in my psyche I am convinced that Lulu's precious 16-year-old body is still my full responsibility. I know I must stop monitoring every morsel she eats, if and when she works out, what goop she puts in her hair, whether her earrings are too heavy for her earlobes, and if she's developing scoliosis from sleeping on too many pillows. I'm driving both her and myself crazy. The good news is I've found that if I channel this anxiety into whether my own wrinkles are getting deeper, if my neck more closely resembles crepe or corduroy, and when a tummy tuck might be in order, I can totally distract myself. Bonus!

Timing is everything. But like everyone else who glibly offers up that cliché, I cannot tell you what the specific timing should be, only warn you of the dire consequences of misfiring. If you hold on too long, you'll end up not only alienating your teen but also engendering tremendous anger and insecurity. If you let go too soon, she could make the kind of legendary bad choices that Lifetime movies are based on—with you starring as the major architect of the disaster. You will have to let your instincts guide you (assuming your rebellious teen hasn't blown them up in the freedom struggle).

This transfer of power—ceding control over the body of your teen—is the central objective of adolescence. But that doesn't make it any less painful, particularly when you are trying your darnedest to deny that any of this adolescent horror is happening. Although I'm a big fan of totalitarian parental control through the first decade of life, history shows that

TALES FROM POST-TEENS ● ● ● ● ● ● ● ● ●

Ahhhh, the tattoo. One day I woke up and decided that getting a tattoo would be a great idea. My best friend at the time, who was only slightly less retarded than me, came with me and got a belly button ring. I walked into the tattoo parlor, looked up on the wall, picked a big wolf howling at the moon, and said, "Put that to the right of my pubic hair." How could I be so dumb as to pick a wolf howling at the moon to tattoo onto my sweet, perfect 15-year-old skin? I even had to pull my pants down in front of a gross old weirdo so he could etch the tattoo next to my privates.

The funny thing is, when I first got it, I loved it. I thought it was, like, the coolest thing ever. By the time I got to college I realized how fucking lame it was. Several boyfriends were shocked when they climbed into bed with me, only to discover a giant wolf hiding in my underpants. To make matters worse, in the past ten years, clothes have become much more low-cut. The location of my tattoo is so 1990s—a pair of high-cut panties would cover it, but a pair of cute little low-riders lets the wolf pop his head out. My best friend pulled her belly ring out two years later and had a tiny little scar, but I have been staring at my huge ugly tattoo for ten years. To this day, I don't know if my mom knows about it because I've never been able to bring myself to tell her. Actually, she probably knows but avoids the topic. Poor thing.

colonialism is not a sustainable system. It ends up creating a super-crabby second-class citizenry who resent the hell out of you and long to smother you in your sleep. Keep that in mind and learn to experience the freedom (for you!) of letting go.

2

Mouth and Lip Disorders of Early Adolescence

ABOUT THE SPLIT SECOND YOUR CHILD TURNS 12 (OR possibly 11, if you're the lucky parent of an early achiever), you'll start experiencing a lot of attitude within the four walls of your formerly peaceful abode. This may take you completely by surprise, as it often manifests itself in response to . . . absolutely nothing.

You will be driving home from church, for instance, and all of a sudden your sweet daughter will scream, "Can you *stop* jerking the brake every time we come to a *light?? Jesus Christ!!*" If you make the colossal blunder of commenting that it's not nice to take the Lord's name in vain on the way home from a religious ceremony, you will doubtless be subjected to another verbal assault dissecting:

   a. your own tendency to swear and use the J.C. words in
     vain.

   b. your heartless cruelty in making her go to church in the
     first place when you *know* she's completely exhausted
     and this was her *one and only* day to sleep in, and how
     Christian is *that*?

   c. your *idiotic* driving style, which is making her feel *com-
     pletely* nauseous and ready to *throw up*.

Once at home she flees up to her room, only to bound
down two minutes later with a sunny smile, begging for waf-
fles. Huh? You chalk it up to a hormone-fueled brain mal-
function and assume that everything is okay.

Everything is not okay.

In fact, it's going to get exponentially worse, with ex-
changes like this occurring on a daily if not hourly basis, until you want to hurl yourself in front of a truck. Now, it's a
given that at this stage your child is going to want to fight
with you about anything and everything. It's your job to figure what's worth fighting about; otherwise, you simply will
not be able to outlast your kid in this battle of wills. Teens are
young and fresh and aching to mix it up over any issue at all.
You are old and stale and aching to mix up nothing but a
cocktail. The odds are seriously against you. So when an outburst starts, take a huge breath and stop and listen to what is
actually being said, rather than reacting to the extreme preju-
dice with which your teen is saying it.

For instance, in the previous example, your daughter's not
talking about *anything*. She's venting. Your particular driving
style has not proven to be an assault on her senses for the
previous twelve years; it's unlikely that it now constitutes virtual child abuse. There is no reason to respond to this diatribe. Let it go.

Many parents feel that when their kids get vicious, they are duty-bound to respond and shut down that nasty attitude. Good luck with that. In my experience, you are duty-bound to protect the sanctity of your household—a task that is going to be infinitely easier if you ignore about 95 percent of the provocative posturing of your teen. Now, I know it's hard to walk away from a cavalcade of insults. But if you value your sanity, you *must*.

Pretend you're in my beloved Philadelphia, where they boo Santa Claus and pelt referees from the stands. Develop your own bit of atty-tude.

THE NO-FEAR FACTOR

You've probably seen the "No Fear" bumper stickers on the back of cars and wondered what that phrase means, much as I'm bewildered by the "One day at a time" message. (What's the alternative? Two days at a time? A half-day at a time?) "No Fear," I'm convinced, is an underground code for what teens experience when they look at us, their parents. It's why they feel free to be defiant, sassy, and insolent—because they have No Fear that we're going to whack them.

"No Fear" is something brand new in parenting. When we were growing up, you knew intuitively, if not experientially, that your dad was perfectly capable of knocking you into next week if you talked back to him. My dad had a deeply worn old razor strop and whenever one of the eight of us got a bit fresh, he would head for the bathroom, unclasp the strop from his towel rack, loop it in half, and walk back into the room, smacking it crisply against his palm. (He never once used it on us, but never once did I believe that it was out of the realm of possibility.) My mom didn't have the heart

AGONIZING EXAMPLE

When she got to be about 13, Cecily became so mouthy and defiant, her mom decided to remove all the CDs and DVDs from her room while she was at school. That night, Cecily discovered her stuff was gone. Outraged, she screamed at her mom, "You can't just come in my room and go through all my stuff!"

"I certainly can!" her mom retorted furiously. "This is my house!"

"We don't even own this house—it's a rental!" Cecily screamed back. "Now stay out of my room!"

At this point, her mom marched in the room and started to take away Cecily's cell phone. Cecily reached out and shoved her mom, her mom shoved her back, and a wild pushing/wrestling/arm-squeezing fracas ensued. Cecily's dad marched in and separated the two panting, sobbing combatants. Cecily fled out the front door and disappeared, barefoot, into the wintry night. Twenty minutes later, Cecily's mom was frantic with worry, pacing around the porch, peering into the darkness, hoarse from shouting Cecily's name. Cecily's dad wasn't panicked because the house is in a small country town and he knew she couldn't have gone far.

"She'll get cold and come in," he said logically.

Cecily's mom walked around the yard for the tenth time, looked up in the apple tree, and saw Cecily crouching high in the branches, mad as a hornet and cold as ice. She pleaded with her to come down, then begged her husband

(continues)

(continued)

to go out and make her come down, but he said Cecily would come in when she was good and ready. A couple minutes later, a frosty but no less infuriated Cecily stomped in the front door and fled up to her room without a word. Cecily's mom broke down in tears and spent the rest of the night in bed with a massive headache. Cecily's dad poured himself a big scotch and wondered how the hell he was going to make it through the next five years.

or heft to be threatening but she was prone to administering a searing snip to the skull to get our attention, dispensing a dozen little rapid-fire smacks to our mouths if we got too sassy with her, or pulling us by our ears to move us somewhere we were resisting going. Back in the day, parents didn't feel bad about using corporal punishment to keep you in line, and they couldn't get arrested for it, either. They knew—and you knew—that you'd asked for it and were very likely to get it.

Today, we don't hit our kids. And I'm sure that's a step in the correct, nonviolent direction. It's also a step right off the cliff of contempt because, let's face it: Fear is a great motivator. If you don't believe it, enlist in the Army and see how fast a drill sergeant will use fear to change your snotty, entitled, sorry-ass attitude.

But I'm compelled to say that if you haven't been smacking your child all along, it's too late to start now. Teens will react very, very badly—and because they're big enough to fight back, things can quickly escalate to a full-scale brawl. In fact, it's probably not a good idea to use *any* form of physical discipline with your teen. For one thing, you're likely to get your ass kicked. For another, in our modern age, all physical touch can be perceived as an assault.

TALES FROM POST-TEENS • • • • • • • • •

I got caught drinking in high school and was suspended from school for a week. They were going to prosecute me, but my father is a lawyer and he challenged the school board and got the entire policy changed so kids could go to an alcohol awareness class and do about a million hours of community service rather than getting a permanent felony on their record. A couple months later, I got drunk again: I was walking home and the cops arrested me for underage drinking. My father came to the police station, bailed me out, and was so furious at me after everything he'd gone through for me the first time, he punched me right in the chest. He'd never hit me before and he never hit me again, but I have to admit, I earned that one.

Yes, our kids have "No Fear." That's probably a great leap forward in parenting, although in my research, many teens can recount a once-in-extreme-circumstances-swat that really got their attention. In any event, it's important that you model a hands-to-yourself attitude. Use your words (remember, as few of them as possible) and learn the underrated pleasure of strategic retreat.

How Can I Miss You
If You Won't Go Away?

In early adolescence, it's entirely possible that you have no perspective on your teen; he just seems like a mutant form of

And More ● ● ● ● ● ● ● ● ● ● ● ● ● ● ●

If there were one thing I regret from my teen years, it would be telling my mom to "shut the hell up." She slapped me in the face, which I absolutely deserved, and I never spoke to her like that again.

your beloved child. This is a normal development—after all, it's hard to see the forest when all the trees are falling on you. Indeed, some days it almost seems as if your teen is purposely picking fights with you. That's because he or she is.

It's an unpleasant truth that living with a teen means your daily exposure to hostility is going to skyrocket. Right now, two opposing forces are locked in a war for supremacy over your teen's brain, smacking his psyche back and forth like a pinball. On the one hand, he wants to be left utterly alone, which accounts for the doors slammed in your face, the lockjaw that sets in when you ask an intrusive question like *How are you doing, honey?* and the shuddering rejection of any physical sign of affection you're naive enough to attempt. And yet, the minute you slump away as vociferously requested, she will go out of her way to engage you in a screaming contest over whether she may stay up until midnight to watch the *Law & Order* marathon. You can't believe this topic is even under discussion, since you've outlawed TV on school nights for years, and she goes to bed at 10 P.M. Yet earlier in the evening, she picked a similar fight over your abusive choice of dinner entrée: *You made BEEF strips? Why don't you just serve me FRESH BLOOD!!!* Then she went ballistic when you asked her to turn down her music so the ceiling didn't vibrate from the bass tones.

TALES FROM POST-TEENS • • • • • • • • •

We have three girls in our family and of course, we used to fight a lot. My dad had this unbelievable ability to completely ignore us and read the paper in the midst of all our screaming and fighting. Even if we started yelling directly at him, he would just rattle the paper and pull it up higher over his face. I hated that! My sisters and I used to complain about how emotionally unavailable he was and we felt super-sorry for ourselves for having such a remote, distancing father. But now that I'm grown, my dad and I have these amazing conversations and I realize he's very easy to engage. He just couldn't handle our screaming blitzes and protected himself by refusing to participate in the hysteria. My mom should have tried that.

Your son, on the other hand, will likely resort to the time-honored guerrilla tactics of subversion. He won't pitch a fit when you ask him to turn the music down; he'll just slowwwwly keep turning his music up, day after day, until it's once again a deafening roar from the third floor. He won't argue with you about homework; he will simply forget to bring it home. He won't plead and scream about going out when he's grounded; he'll slyly slip out the back door. My stepson became so devious when he was about 13 (and 14, 15, 16, 17, and 18), my husband had to literally sit on him to prevent him from stealing out of the house at night. Boys at this age have a very difficult time articulating their feelings; instead, they act out and sneak out.

Girls are hysterical and in your face; boys are subtle and unabashedly defiant. Both are utterly confounding for parents, at least at this stage of denial. If she wants to be left alone, why does she keep engaging you in these epic show-downs over idiotic battles she knows she can't win? If he wants to be trusted, why does he keep breaking every treaty you've both agreed to? Who does he think he is—Iran?

The answer to these questions is that teenagers are a walk-ing, talking contradiction in terms. They want to be exactly like the kids in *Real World*, free of you and all your insanely protective restrictions. But they are also saddled with annoy-ing emotions of deep love and attachment to you that they wholeheartedly wish would disappear. And so, teens act out a primal battle between the different parts of *themselves:* the lit-tle child and the emerging adult. You are merely the unfortu-nate target in the middle of a psychological tug-of-war.

Keep this in mind the next time the floodgates open and you're bathed in animosity for the crime of trying to put din-ner on the table. Try to maintain some empathy for what your child is working her way through, even when it appears to be your last nerve ending. When in pointless conflict with your teen, establish some distance.* Take a long walk, or lock yourself in the bathroom and turn on sports talk radio to blank out all brain activity (my husband's methodology). Don't come out until the shelling has stopped.

*This is generally easier for fathers than for mothers. Mothers tend to be the ones tending to the nitty-gritty details of a teenager's life, which means there are many more points of contact—and op-portunities for conflict. When things heat up, dads need to quickly step in to neutralize the situation (always take Mom's side, Pop) so mothers aren't buried alive in teen defiance and can disengage.

The Buckwheat Stops Here

Remember when you were growing up and you ate whatever your mom served for dinner? Banish that image from your mind;

it will only torment you. We've given our kids far too much control over what they eat since birth and hence produced a generation of finicky, overfed, picky eaters. Research has proven that if you don't introduce children to certain foods by the time they are 5, they will never develop a taste for them. (This theory holds true until they are in college and some hottie introduces them to shitake mushrooms and wasabi. Before you know it, your picky eater will be tossing back oyster shots like Pez in a frenzy to impress. But under your mundane influence? Never.)

Expanding your kids' palate when they are teens is well-nigh impossible. They will scream bloody murder if you insist they "just try it"; you stand a better chance of getting them to yodel or tidy up their closets. The more extreme fantasy that you can somehow get teens to choose healthy foods *on their own* is deep-fat-fried pie in the sky.

Kids love junk food. Salty, sweet, greasy, carbonated, loaded with preservatives, and in colors not found anywhere in the natural world—yeah, baby! That doesn't mean you have to have junk food in your house, but don't expect your teen to abstain when he or she is not around you and presented with the opportunity to gorge. You can only do what you can do: Present a healthy model for good eating choices ("Put down that French fry and back away slowly from the nacho bar, dude") and stock your refrigerator with fresh fruits and vegetables. If you avoid processed foods in all their many, many disguises (what the hell happened to yogurt, for instance?), you'll be on the road to recovery from revolting food choices. Of course, there is a school of thought that proposes the more you deny kids all forms of junk, the more intense their cravings for junk become. That's the theory Lulu is constantly trying to sell me, but I'm not buying it.

Of course, once you lay down the food law, you will have to contend with being the no-fun household, the nutritious one to be avoided at all costs. That was my household growing up, although with eight kids my mom was probably thrilled not to have a single extra child underfoot. My best friend Nancy lived in a paradise of potato chips, Popsicles, and peppermint patties and we hung out at her house all the time. Of course, I want my daughter's friends to hang out at our house but I have a genetic predisposition toward eschewing salt- and sweet-laden snacks and that makes for less than ideal hanging-out conditions. I'm trying to find some kind of middle ground, like stockpiling snacks on days of visitation only.

In truth, I'm not very flexible around food issues; the best I can do is try to foreshorten my lectures and ditch all my enlightening statistics on weight, calories, trans fats, and additives. Unfortunately, I'm burdened by the belief that one's job as a parent is to make sure your children eat properly and develop healthy habits. Isn't it? Yet certainly as they grow older, most teens' response to any counsel on what to eat is likely to be: *Shove it*. And with each passing Twinkie, the food struggle becomes increasingly less productive. When it comes to dispensing an open buffet of unwanted dietary advice, we over-invested parents probably should *just shove it*.

THE EXCRUCIATING
EMBARRASSMENT OF YOU

If you're going to make it through the next six or seven years of adolescence, you need to understand a few more things about this new relationship you're entering with your teen. Here's a useful metaphor: Living with a teenager is like being in a seven-year audition with Simon Cowell on *American Idol*. The only difference is, Simon has moments when he is almost kind, or not purposely cruel. Teenagers, however, are loath to break character and show you they love you because they

TALES FROM POST-TEENS • • • • • • • • •

My biggest fights with my parents were about food. My mom was a psycho food fanatic, wanting me to eat healthy—no sweets, nothing I actually liked. She sent me to school with disgusting food that I immediately threw out and replaced with other stuff I bought at the school's cafeteria. We had to drink milk at every meal. Needless to say, it was terrible. We sometimes refused to eat for a while, especially when she made disgusting meat loaf. Every mealtime was a battle.

can't afford to. If they let you know how much they care, they'd be giving you a leg up in this hideous struggle called growing up. It would underscore the reality that they still depend on you for transportation, Doritos, Air Force Ones, unconditional love—and, oh yeah, cash. That dependence (both emotional and financial) is what they do not want to admit because then they might be tempted to spend time with you, which would be hugely pathetic.

Thus, they must distance themselves in every way. Mostly, that means criticizing everything about you. From the way you part your hair to the way you chew your food. (Parental mastication somehow becomes both mesmerizing and mortifying the minute a kid hits 13.) From the style of jeans you are uncool enough to wear to the fact that an old fart like you is even wearing jeans at all. Literally *everything* about you becomes a supreme embarrassment to your children. This agony is only compounded by the indisputable fact that you share the same genetic material. Thus, there is a chance, no matter how infinitesimal, that way out there in the future they may turn out to be like you in some completely grotesque way. Deep down, they realize that you have (sneakily, when they were far too young to resist) infected them with all kinds of habits, beliefs, and values that are in there, waiting to come seeping out and turn them into . . . YOU!

Aaaaauuuuugghhhhhhh!

Faced with that possibility, they *have* to reject you. Otherwise, how will they ever be able to be themselves?

It's not pleasant to anticipate, but if you can achieve a modicum of understanding of what your children are trying to achieve with their wholesale repudiation of you, it may make it a tad less painful. In other words, it's not *personal*. It's the process of differentiation. Take comfort in the fact that you *are* in their genetic material, you *are* that voice inside their head they detest, and in your sneaky way, you *have* made your mark on your child. So unlike Simon, they can't kick you off the show, no matter how badly they may want to.

Breaking Up Is Hard to Do

Get out your hankies. Because of all the changes adolescence brings, this aspect is the most heartrending.

Your child is going to break up with you.

She's not going to crawl into your lap or cuddle up with you. He's not going to tunnel under your covers in the morning or throw himself into your arms when he comes home from school. You are about to embark on an affection starvation diet. And since this is nothing you agreed to when you brought their adorable little butts into the world, you may find yourself struggling to accept the deprivation.

Think of it this way: It's like a great relationship that is morphing from an overwhelmingly intense love affair to a mutually beneficial friendship in which you care a lot about the other person but don't feel responsible for his daily routines,

TALES FROM POST-TEENS ● ● ● ● ● ● ● ● ●

I think talking back was my form of rebellion, my way to assert my own independence. Or maybe it was that I was (and continue to be) so much like my mom. When she did something that annoyed me, I realized it was probably something I did myself. And if I didn't like it when she did it, then I wasn't going to like it when I did it. I felt like I had to fight like hell not to become her in any way. (Or maybe I was just a snot and karma is going to kick my ass when my own daughter turns 15.)

sniffly nose, or poor posture. You are not grieved or panicked when that person isn't around, nor afflicted with the kind of longing that makes you feel like half your heart is missing when the beloved is gone.

That change is starting to happen now. So over the next few years, you are going to have to learn not to stalk your child. You're going to have to give him his space, and allow her to experiment with ridiculous hairdos and appalling makeup without saying *a word*. Your child's withdrawal from a physical relationship with you is natural, but of course the pain is exacerbated since he doesn't want to walk, talk, or live like you, either. Needless to say, it's painful to be with somebody who finds you repulsive. When you feel like your teen is trying to negate everything about you, mimic something you do that you know drives him or her crazy. Making fun of yourself is an oddly powerful tactic, and it'll completely disarm your little critic. It might even make him laugh.

As you back out of the fray, do continue to seek out any opportunity you can for closeness. I am queen of the surreptitious sofa snuggle and will gladly sit through one lame sitcom after another merely to have Lulu tucked in beside me. My husband loves to play basketball with his boys, if only for the chance to sling an arm over their shoulders for a brief, manly hug afterward.

If you're not too busy fighting over parenting, you might even consider reaching out to your mate for the comfort and affection you're not getting from your kid anymore. Research shows that empty-nesters are far less stressed, more content, and have a lot more sex than parents of teens, who lead the pack of the sexually deprived. Things are looking up!

AGONIZING EXAMPLE

Jackie is a single mom, and her son's dad is such a deadbeat she has had to bring Alex up entirely on her own. When her son was small, she learned to do all the boy things; she played with dinosaurs, trucks, and Star Wars characters, collected bugs and lizards, made mud pies, and became adept at video games. She went to every one of Alex's soccer, basketball, and football games; learned how to pitch a tent; and earned multiple Scout badges. She was awesome.

But when Alex turned 14, he began to block her out of his life and shut himself up in his room. She called me on the verge of hysteria." What's wrong with him? He can't stand to be around me! He hates me!" Working herself into a total panic, she was sure he was going through some kind of mental illness or giant depression. Finally, she went to a family counselor—who told her that Alex was acting normally and gently suggested that perhaps she should get out more and develop a life that didn't entirely revolve around her son.

3

IMPENDING ASSAULTS ON PARENTAL SANITY

REMEMBER WHEN IT FIRST OCCURRED TO YOU THAT everything in your parenting world was about to change? You were driving the minivan, and your charming 10-year-old and her friends begged you to turn on the radio. You flipped on the station they liked, got a great beat, the kids started singing, and you were bopping along with the groove, humming the chorus. All of a sudden you realize the words in the chorus are literally "To the window, to the wall, 'til the sweat rolls down my balls. . . . "

What?

From the back of the minivan, your genial carload of prepubescent girls continues singing these lyrics at the top of their little lungs. You lunge for the dial and click out of that song to another radio station, where some breathy woman is extolling the alluring beauty of "my humps, my humps, my lovely lady lumps."

Ewwwww!

You frantically punch the dial again and thank God, no more nasty lyrics. Instead, you've tuned into a "Booty Call," where callers try to talk their unsuspecting lovers into bagging work to come home and have sex. You hear the little girl in pigtails who lives next door telling your daughter, "Shhhh! I want to see if she can get him to come home and do it."

What the . . . ?!

Welcome to the wonderful world of Teen Pop Culture. This is what our kids are exposed to every day and if you think I'm exaggerating, tune into any top morning show, or go to *lyrics.com* and download the words to almost any current hit song. (Memo to folks at work: Erase this from your cache immediately because you could probably be fired for downloading porn.)

This is why a lot of people don't allow their kids to listen to pop music, and I don't blame them one bit. I didn't do it soon enough and once the horse is out of the barn, it's hard to rein it back in. Plus, my daughter loves to dance and she's addicted to R&B and hip-hop music; I simply didn't have the heart to outlaw it. Hence, I now live with a posse of 50 Cent, Outkast, T.I., Usher, Ludacris, Lil' Jon, and a whole host of other Lils'. I do insist the station has to be changed when I hear lyrics that totally gross me out. But Lulu's got all the songs on her iTunes anyhow, so I don't know whom I think I'm fooling.

POP! GOES THE CULTURE

If you want to control the insidious incursion of pop culture into your household, you'll have to start early and religiously monitor your kid's access to television, movies, magazines, videos, music, radio, and the Internet. Not getting cable is a good start, since almost everything on TV is smut-packed and adult in content, although your husband may feel sport-deprived (and smut-deprived) by this tactic. Parental controls are an option, although the vast majority of older kids can figure a way around them. Refusing to allow kids to have tel-evisions, computers, and radios in their bedrooms is essential since anything in *their* rooms is out of *your* control. Period.

With consistent effort, you may be able to exert a great deal of control over what your elementary school child is exposed to, but as he or she becomes a tween, the struggle becomes exponentially harder. For starters, he or she is likely to start rebelling against your fascist, authoritarian regime. (Go Mom!) You'll have to be very careful about who your child's friends are and where they hang out, since it's unlikely other parents will share your same resolve. (A guidance counselor told me that a huge source of sex "education" for middle schoolers occurs at sleepovers where one child will introduce the rest to the glories of Internet porn. Now there's a fun party idea!) Additionally, you'll have to muzzle older siblings since they are notorious for introducing younger sibs to all the cool new things they've dis-covered, like pot, gangsta rap, MTV, and R-rated slasher flicks.

All in all, controlling your child's exposure to pop culture is a daunting task that becomes more quixotic with every year. You'll have to be passionately committed and realize your kids will want you to *be* committed for the crime of keeping them . . . *"so sheltered and protected and completely out of it!!"* It's likely your teen will feel like he is missing out on all the cool stuff that's going on and blame you for making him look lame in the eyes of his friends. That's actually okay, but the struggle is not going to be pretty. In the midst of all that spewing teen outrage, many parents will give up the battle to hold the VJs at bay.

If you do end up caving and find your household overrun with Soulja Boys and Gossip Girls, remember that at least you fought the good fight and plenty of other parents are down there grinding with you. Bolster your confidence by recalling with fondness how much your parents hated the idiotic TV shows and druggie, satanic music you listened to, and you turned out okay. Sorta.

Fighting over pop culture and believing you are going to permanently control how much of it your child will ingest is one of the surest signs that you're in the denial stage of parenting an adolescent. Good times.

WORDS OF WISDOM

I've discovered a fail-safe way to ruin your teen's enjoyment of hip-hop, but you have to be willing to totally humiliate yourself to accomplish it. A couple months ago, in a moment of inexplicable adventurousness, I decided to take hip-hop dance classes at my fitness club. I thought I was pretty good and came home and showed off some of my new dance moves to Lulu. I demonstrated the snake, in which I look like a contortionist, and my Beyonce booty-bouncing routine. Lulu was laughing so hard she almost threw up, and immediately took my photo on her cell phone and sent it to all her friends. (Thank God she hadn't learned how to post videos on YouTube.) But when I started playing the Black Eyed Peas in the car and singing along to all of Ludacris's songs, her mirth died. She became so horrified at my embracing her music, she actually urged me to change the station to NPR. I feel a tiny bit guilty for co-opting her culture and figure I've contaminated hip-hop for her forever. Oh darn.

TALES FROM POST-TEENS • • • • • • • •

My older brothers turned me on to rap when I was about 9, and I got addicted to it. They'd burn me CDs of all the latest rappers, and I was pretty hip for a kid my age. Of course, my mom hated it and she would go on and on about how it was materialistic and misogynistic, but she couldn't stop my older brothers from listening to it. Or me. Rap just seemed real to me in a way that my suburban life didn't. When I got older, I got into alternative music, but rap was my first love.

ROADKILL ON THE
INFORMATION SUPERHIGHWAY

If you want to see anxiety in action, simply say to the parent of a young adolescent, "How do you control your child on the Internet?" Bingo. An instant panic attack mixed with self-recrimination, fear, and cluelessness—about as toxic a cocktail as life shakes up for a parent. Yes, it's a whole new World Wide Web out there and frankly, the challenge of protecting your child on it is more than a bit overwhelming.

As your child moves into adolescence, she will doubtless make the online leap from designing new Barbie outfits to IMing people with hooks like *lilpimp32* and *bootylicious55*. It's times like these that I earnestly wish I were a born-again, home-schoolin', off-the-grid parent at holy war with our society. Instead, I'm another lost sheep with my own wicked addiction to email, trying to figure out how to empower and insulate my kid from technology at the same time.

How much do you know, and can you know, about what your child is doing on the computer? Good question. Despite all the experts telling you to regularly monitor your child's Internet use, I think it's supremely optimistic to think that your skills are going to trump your child's. The entire computer industry is geared toward enabling kids to use technology anywhere and everywhere they want. And it will never stop innovating ways to shove you out of the loop, since this is precisely what its primary consumers, our children, most fervently desire.

I have seen the future, and it is not us. It's them. Our smart-ass kids.

When you read stories of smug parents who claim to be right on top of all their kids' computer activities, take them with a shaker of salt. Don't feel bad because you're not a forensic computer wiz. Be sure to ask who *lilpimp32* is and hope that your teen is telling you the truth, that he's that sweet kid in her church choir. Just don't believe everything she tells you, and don't give in to the feeling that the Internet is too big an issue for you to take on.

Think of the Internet as a *tangible* place, not a virtual one. We wouldn't let our young kids wander around the city by themselves, and it makes every bit as much sense to know where they're going online. Regularly go through their browser caches and look at the sites they have visited under the "History" icon (on a Mac) or hold down the Control key and hit the "H" key (on a PC). Voilà, Hansel and Gretel's online trail! Another tip is to set up bookmarks for favorite sites, to keep surfing to a minimum. Above all, put the computer in a place where you'll be able to casually walk by and see what your kids are doing (a fantastically simple and underrated deterrent to online mischief).

Once a computer gets into your child's bedroom, it'll be off your radar. In fact, many teens sleep with their electronics; laptops and cell phones are quickly becoming the teddy bears of the new millennium. I missed the opportunity for oversight when Lulu's dad gave her a computer and installed it in her bedroom, and I've had nothing but regret ever since. Of course, your teen will resent the hell out of you for any monitoring of his or her computer use and consider it an egregious invasion of privacy.

Boo hoo.

Since you're infringing on your child's privacy, you might also want to consider limiting the time your teen spends on the computer. This limitation will be met with all the outrage of someone losing his ability to walk, but having only an hour or two to spend online per day does not constitute a disability. I've checked with the ADA.

If you feel strong enough, you may also try to involve your teen in conversations about what's appropriate to do online (IM, games, chat, research—ha!) and what's not (illegal downloading and adult sites leap to mind). Give your child accurate statistics about pedophiles trolling social sites (FYI: Researchers found that 3,000-plus known sex offenders had MySpace profiles, and that was just a quick screen of registered, convicted creeps.) Don't be discouraged if your teen cuts you short with a curt "I know all this crap, Mom, and I can take care of myself so *stop lecturing me about it!*"

Of course, your ability to educate your child may be limited by your naiveté, as is mine. One child protection expert suggested this helpful tidbit on educating kids about the downside of social networking: "We should talk frankly to our kids about how online predators operate and what to watch out for." Sadly, my lack of understanding of how predators operate is matched only by my ignorance about what to look out for, or even how to get onto a social networking site. Ask an older sibling, cousin, or trusted babysitter to talk to your child in confidence. Unlike you, kids under 30 live on these sites and can access your child's site and see photos he or she has posted and how much information has been given out. Be absolutely certain your teen has a closed account of friends (but realize kids are famous for letting in friends-of-friends, some of whom might be 40-year-olds). Since my research (unaided by the Internet) has shown that teenagers never hear anything until repeated at least five times, do not let your teen's "reassurance" dissuade you from the lecture or the oversight. Nag on, Mama! Hold that line, Dad!

Then pray a lot. As teens grow older, try to accept the fact that the Internet is their world and they have to learn how to negotiate it under the guidance of age-appropriate rules. Finally, don't forget to have someone look at your system to see how pathetically easy it may be to override every single one of your parental controls.

Big Stupid Clothes / Tiny Trashy Clothes

Somewhere around the age of 12, my stepson Tyler began to want really big t-shirts. We went out and bought him XL shirts that pooled around his shoulders like a poncho, presumably the desired effect. One year later, as I was doing his laundry, I noticed he had graduated into the truly gargantuan sizes and I was physically incapable of folding his 3X shirts, as they were approximately the size of a queen sheet. His pants, likewise, began to get wider and longer, although his actual dimensions hadn't changed much. Inevitably, the bottoms shredded and frayed as he walked on them in the big, clumpy Timberland boots that were also now *de rigueur*.

WORDS OF WISDOM

If you do manage to intercept one of your child's many, many IM conversations, you may find yourself oddly reassured. My husband was trying to print out a budget one night and ended up with twenty-five pages of Lulu's IM conversations that were stupendously boring. We instantly felt better, although deeply frightened for her future as a linguist. This is a very abbreviated version:

Hey.

Hey.

U there?

Duhh.

Lol.

seen rachel?

yeah.

cool.

yeah.

So.

got a test 2morro.

me too

science?

math.

sucks

yeah.

studying?

no.

Lol . . .

gotta go.

Okay

later

sure?
sure
holla back
yeah.
cu . . .
not if i cu first . . .
lol.

What is the *point*? I have no idea, but the content didn't seem life threatening. That was good. Of course, it was eating up valuable studying time. But it's not like Lulu would be working her way through her dissertation if it weren't for IM.

Plus, it's difficult to keep up with the threat of the moment. Teens are notoriously fickle and move from one online activity to the next with blinding speed. One day they're IMing, the next they're MySpacing, the next they're Facebooking. The loyalty factor of teens for any social network is zero, which sort of makes you wonder why companies are paying billions of dollars for them.

If you can bear the tedium, go to the elucidating Web sites *www.noslang.com* and *www.netlingo.com* for help in decoding your own teen's text-messaging and chatting.

I know this style of huge saggy clothing is now so mainstream it hardly bears scrutiny, but I hate it. For one thing, it prevents movement. It's a bit difficult to run when your pants are cinched loosely around your thighs, which I think would be a slight handicap. It's also a terrifically annoying laundry challenge, as one huge pair of pants can easily take up half a load of wash. Finally, with hoodie up and face buried in the gloom of dark cotton, every kid—no matter how geeky or wholesome—can look threatening and thoroughly arrestible. For a lot of boys, that's the highest possible achievement, but it's ironic to see an entire nation of affluent white boys trying so hard to look marginalized.

Apparently, clothing manufacturers are getting all the material for boys' huge clothing from the other sex, as the minimal amount of fabric covering teen girls boggles the mind. The streetwalker look is alive and well in Teen America, and even Preteen America, if the uber-slutty Bratz dolls are any indication. Halter tops are held up with straps made of microfilament. Tummies are on full display since designers brazenly decided to crop the tops while they were dropping the waistline of jeans to the pubic bone. Skirts graze the upper thighs. A visit to any high school might be mistaken for a plumbers' convention, you'll see so many butt cracks on display.

Of course, the mere fact that it's the fashion doesn't mean you need to allow your teen daughter to prance around like one of the Pussycat Dolls. Modesty can be enforced as long as you hold the purse strings to the clothing allowance and don't get sucked in by the vociferous demand for self-expression in clothing. Let's get real. You're not going to wipe out your teen's creativity and individuality by insisting that she cover her boobs and butt, or that he pull up his pants and stop trying to look like a gangster. In fact, I believe it's your duty to intervene when your child is angling for a style that gives people an immediate and visceral bad impression. There's plenty of time for teens to express themselves sartorially when they're in college and out of your sight.

Then again, I am totally in favor of school uniforms for public and private schools alike, so you can see where I stand on the issue of personal expression in clothing. The admissions

TALES FROM POST-TEENS ● ● ● ● ● ● ● ●

Clothes aren't only self-expression for a teen; they're a statement of what group you're in. Nobody on the planet could have made me wear preppy clothes when I was growing up because that's not who I was, and nobody I hung out with dressed that way, either. The kind of clothes you wear lets people know who you are. Parents are clueless about this.

AND MORE ● ● ● ● ● ● ● ● ● ● ● ● ● ●

My mom was always trying to improve my sense of style, which is hopeless for any parent because to a teen, the term "fashionable mother" is like an oxymoron. I remember her constantly telling me that my shirts were too tight. And in hindsight, I think that's probably the lamest thing she could have said. Of course my shirts were too tight. I was 14 and totally jazzed with my little mosquito bites.

director at Lulu's school, which has a hideously unattractive and restrictive uniform (including regulation shirts, pants, skirts, shoes, socks, *and* jackets), meets with about 5,000 kids a year and here's what he has to say on the subject: "Kids are always going to rebel against something. If you give them something rather insignificant like a uniform to protest against, they're going to rebel by wearing the wrong kind of socks. Or trying to get away with not tucking their shirt in. If they have nothing small to oppose, they'll find a way to rebel in larger, more illegal and dangerous ways."

I think he's probably right. Honestly, though, my fervent embrace of uniforms is based more on ending the expensive, time-consuming arms race of buying high-status clothing, keeping things simple on school mornings, and hating to do laundry.

Disgust with big stupid clothes (and tiny slutty clothes) is just gravy.

SAY CHEESE

If you're reading this in preparation for your kid's impending adolescence, not only do you get bonus points for your proactive approach, you'll also have the opportunity to get the last known photos of your happy child. Snap away, quickly! Because about the time your child turns 12, something terrible will happen to his or her face.

It closes. The eyes that used to peer into yours with vivaciousness and joy will lower to half-mast, as apparently too much effort is required to hoist them to eye level. The lips that used to curl upward in a heart-melting smile or pucker into a charming smooch now hang open in a stupor, smirk in contempt, or jut out in an angry pout. Soft-as-petals cheeks turn to cement and eyebrows are raised only to express the utter disbelief that someone as inept as you is allowed to live.

This painful transformation from sunny to sullen is universal, yet it's important to realize it's mostly confined to home. You may be amazed to witness your child in the schoolyard and see the outgoing, happy kid you once knew—only to watch the blinds being drawn in that face as she makes her way to the car and to you, the scourge of her teenage existence. Or perhaps his alienation has infected every aspect of his life and he never snaps out of the personality coma into which he's descended. Don't put him on life support quite yet.

Tales from Post-Teens ● ● ● ● ● ● ● ●

I'm Jewish and at my bat-mitzvah, I was supposed to have a father-daughter dance that's a really big deal in my culture. At the time, I was busy throwing a fit about how the video cameraman we'd hired was overly in my face and being such a nuisance I couldn't enjoy the party. In between my tears came the moment for the long-awaited dance, but I couldn't let my aggravation go. Now every time I watch the video that idiotic cameraman made, I have to watch myself looking disgusted to be dancing with my father. I regret the fact that I couldn't just enjoy the moment, as it was obviously supposed to be a very special one. I'm so ashamed I turned it into an ungrateful-daughter moment.

It's a *phase*. Pull out your old family albums and look at photos from the bygone era of your own adolescence. It's highly likely you look disgruntled and glum in every frame. Camera and film marketing experts will tell you there is a predictable and precipitous drop-off in the number of photographs that parents take of their children beginning at age 12 and lasting through high school. Is this because teenagers suddenly refuse to allow you to take their photo, or is it that you gradually lose interest in taking yet another photo of a person glaring at you through the lens?

Yes.

When your baby is born, you can't have enough photos of the Precious Bundle. *Your* child. But the entire process of adolescence is about your child becoming his or her own property. Allow him to scowl away, but don't stop capturing his essence on film, if for no other reason than you can use it to embarrass the hell out of him in later years. (Twenty years

ago, my father, in an utterly unprecedented show of attention, put together an entire slide show of my most hideous
teen moments to share with my new fiancé.) Plan ahead.

CONDITIONS VARY:
THESE RULES MAY NOT APPLY . . .

When you're first starting out on the forced march of adolescence, it's important (and possibly nausea-inducing) to realize that you're in it for a long haul. Despite your natural
desire to get a handle on things, there are precious few rules
that will hold fast and true through the upcoming years. One
is that you really can't hit your children, no matter how
much they truly deserve it and would probably benefit from
it. Another is that you can't drink before breakfast, no matter
how much you truly deserve it and would probably benefit
from it.

Other than these two strictures, most everything is in flux.

In the denial stage, it may be difficult to realize how profoundly your child will change over the next five years—and
how remarkably your parenting methods will bend, stretch,
and even snap to accommodate the growth of your teen. You
must constantly consider if your rules are age-appropriate
and reflective of your teen's ability to think about anything
beyond the next episode of *The O.C.* It requires perspective to
determine if you're giving in too early or holding out too
long, and thus you may be tempted to ask other parents for
guidance. Which brings me to my next point: Before you dive
into the advice pool, be keenly aware of how other people's
counsel is making you feel.

Like every other parent of a teen, you're likely to be desperate for help and empathy. Sometimes this will lead you to

the wrong source (meaning, anybody whose child is older, younger, or not as deeply screwed up as yours). If you talk to parents whose child is older, they are likely to give you advice that will make you feel like Stalin for not allowing your child comparable freedom. When Lulu was 12, for instance, I asked my friend Tammi in California for advice about appropriate bedtimes in middle school. She was trying to decide whether to allow her 15-year-old to sleep with her boyfriend in the house and suggested I think about when I was going to offer Lulu birth control. Not really very helpful. If you give advice to people whose kids are younger than yours, you're likely to offer similarly inappropriate counsel and they'll look at you as if you possess all the parenting skills of Britney Spears. Seek counsel from a parent whose kid is a model of overachievement when yours is scrabbling for Cs, and you're going to feel like both you and your kid are total losers.

Asking for help in parenting your teen is a lot like seeking guidance on menopause and aging. Sometimes you're ready to hear about what's in store for you and sometimes it's better simply to face the horror as it happens. In short, don't borrow trouble. And try not to dispense it, either.

No Free Passes

My friend Rebecca called me the other day. She couldn't wait to tell me about our mutual friend Ann Marie who (unlike us) is a patient, saintly mother. Ann Marie's two daughters are younger than ours, and she's watched in horror as we fight with our daughters and they pull the kind of crap teenage girls do. Like all of us, Ann Marie fully believed that she would be spared the horrors of adolescence due to her excellent parenting skills.

But that morning her daughters, ages 13 and 10, got up late and missed the school bus. Both Ann Marie and her husband Peter had important morning meetings and neither was able to drive the girls to school, half an hour away. They told the girls they could stay home as long as they promised to do their homework, read, and not watch TV. The girls earnestly promised to be good as gold. But as the parents were racing off to work, Peter overheard his studious older daughter telling the younger daughter, "Of course we're going to watch TV. How are they going to know? They won't be here, you moron!" Peter moved to the solution and sabotaged the entire cable system before he left for work, but Ann Marie was unhinged by this defiance and deception in her previously docile older daughter.

As Ann Marie anxiously told the story on the train to work, Rebecca burst out laughing.

"Did you think Betty and I were exaggerating about what it's like to raise teenagers?" she asked Ann Marie in mock outrage. "Or did you just think we were slacker moms and it would never happen to somebody as earnest and hardworking as you?"

Parents can be forgiven for believing that somehow they are going to be spared the bullet of obnoxious adolescence because of their great sensitivity, caring, and effort. That's perfectly normal—and delusional. Because no matter what kind of paragon of virtue you are, you're unlikely to escape the agony of adolescence with your teenager. Try to take comfort in the fact that at least we're all in this together.

Stage 2: Anger

AGES 14–15,
THE FEUDAL AGE

OF ALL THE EMOTIONS ASSOCIATED WITH PARENTING an adolescent, anger is king. I don't think it's necessarily because you're mad all the time—well, actually it is because you're mad all the time. But anger, in my psychological repertoire, is the default emotion for many of the others I would prefer not to feel, like fear, rejection, and sadness. Somehow, it seems more powerful to throw something against a wall or flip somebody off. Okay, now that *my* personality confessional is out of the way, let's talk about *your* anger.

Unless you are Mother Teresa (in which case, you wouldn't have had marital relations, wouldn't have had kids, and wouldn't now be suffering teen behavior that makes working in the slums of Calcutta seem like a super-relaxing alternative)—well, it's likely your life has been filled with moments of anger.

When someone stole your toy in kindergarten, it made you angry. When someone stole your boyfriend in eighth grade, it made you angry. So now when your child steals himself away from you, it's going to make you angry. You're dealing with loss, and losing things makes people mad. That's natural—but remember that natural can also mean painful. (Need I mention childbirth?)

Adolescence is all about control issues, and losing control likewise makes people angry. Time after time, you will mutter to yourself, *"But WHY? WHY do I have to let him wear that ridiculous knit cap that makes him look like a terrorist/quit baseball/give up piano/fail history/eat handfuls of French fries/never say her prayers/stay up late/watch crap TV/make friends with losers/stop reading? WHY?"*

You used to be able to control almost everything your child ate, drank, wore, watched, played with, learned, and said. You were the parent; that was your job. Now, with absolutely no warning, you're supposed to embark on a systematic plan to turn full operational control over to the kid. It's like Bill Gates being asked to turn Microsoft over to Carmen Electra. But turn it over you must.

So, you're upset. This chapter deals with the righteousness of that anger and its ultimate futility. Eventually, you are going to have to accept that your child is growing up and leaving (keep in mind the long-term goal of separation). While you have every reason to resent your new role as the punching bag in your child's boxing match with life, it's important to look for ways to move beyond anger. To shorten the stage. To preserve what's left of your equanimity and stomach lining.

Laughing helps.

4

The Minefields

THERE IS NO E-Z PASS ON THE TURNPIKE OF TEEN parenting. The road is fast. It's tricky to maneuver. And unlike Germans on the autobahn, you're not zipping along in a superbly engineered vehicle designed for speed. You're plodding along in your same old creaky personality, trying desperately to keep up with the wild mood swings of your teen.

The older your child gets, the faster things go, and emotions are no exception. If you have ADD, congratulations! You're way ahead of the curve in coping with your kid's schizoid personality. And if you're manic-depressive, you might want to consider tutoring other parents since clearly, you know the drill.

It's morning and your teen is in a chasm of depression. School is completely overwhelming and she's sure her science teacher is out to get her. She has a meltdown trying to print out her English paper, refuses to eat breakfast, and you have to threaten to take away her iPod to get her to choke down a banana. Some critical piece of sports gear has gone missing, and all hell breaks loose as she stumbles around the house trying to find it. As she's walking out the door, you remind her of her dental appointment this afternoon and she screams at you that she hates her life. And you.

For the remainder of the day (in between working your butt off to earn a living to sustain the lifestyle your teen loathes), you make a full-scale plan to get your child into therapy, schedule a talk with the despised science teacher and guidance counselor, download ten pages of information about artistic and creative activities she might like, and generally feel drained, anxious, and sad. Filled with trepidation, you pick her up after school, only to watch her bound off the bus, laughing and shouting goodbyes to her friends, then plop into the car and exclaim, "Hi Mommy! Can I change the radio station?"

Girls are extreme practitioners of the mood swing, but my advice to parents of both sexes is: Don't assign any more importance to their moods than you have to. Practice deep-listening skills and then, total amnesia. A spirit of compassionate empathy goes a long way, if you can manage to keep your comments and reactions to a minimum.

A. Path of Maximum Agony

You hate your hair? Then why did we spend $120 getting it cut that way when I told you layers wouldn't work? Maybe if you didn't put so much conditioner in it, it wouldn't be so limp. Listen, why not try to pull it back in a ponytail and then. . . . Don't walk away from me, young lady! I'm trying to help!

B. New and Improved Agony

You hate your hair? Bummer.

THE PERFECT STORM

If you've ever doubted that God has a twisted sense of humor, consider this fact. Precisely when your daughter or son is going bonkers with hormones, the woman of the family— the stabilizer, the one who's actually interested in communication and emotional understanding, the very glue holding the family together—will suddenly begin losing estrogen and going off the rails. It's a bizarre confluence of events that results in epic domestic turbulence and almost makes you feel sorry for the man of the house, pinned between these two irrational forces of nature. To cope with an adolescent, a woman needs every ounce of calm she can dig down and muster. Instead, she starts sweating like a sumo wrestler, can't sleep, puts on three inches of belly fat, and feels enraged about anything that thwarts her—like the universe, for instance. Teens respond to this situation with keen understanding, meaning they will try to light the fuse of their formerly peace-loving mother as frequently as possible.

There are many medical solutions to this problem, but most will kill you. Creative lifestyle changes, like moving to New Zealand or joining Cirque de Soleil, are exciting alternatives, although most women in menopause do not possess the requisite financial or physical flexibility. Clearly, these options are not for everyone.

One simple thing I've found helpful is to watch reruns of *That 70s Show* and witness Claire Forman's progression

My mom was 37 when she had me, so about the time I turned 14 she was going through menopause. Obviously, being a guy I didn't realize it at the time, but I remember her fanning herself all the time, yanking at her collar like it was choking her, and wandering around the house sleepless in the middle of the night, muttering to herself. She never screamed or anything, but she did start crying a lot. Like, all the time. She started going to church almost every day and would come home, cry for a while, and then get on with things. And every time I would yell at her about something, she would burst into tears. At the time I thought it was really manipulative, but now I feel sort of badly that I was such a shit to her.

through menopause. Basically, she lashes out at her family, throws things out the window, attacks innocent bystanders, and screams at everyone in range. It's wonderful therapy.

I'm Not Shouting, You're Shouting!

Until you fully grasp that conflict is precisely what your teen wants, it's likely that things are going to get A LOT LOUDER around your house. This is totally your teen's fault, of course. However, one thing every angry parent needs to realize is the part *you* play in the decibel debacle. Remember when you used to fight with your college roommate about whose music was going to prevail, and you both kept cranking up the volume until your eardrums were vibrating like tissue paper, as James Brown collided head-on with Pink Floyd? It's like that. The more your teen yells at you, the more likely you are to yell back, which will cause him to holler louder, which will hack you off and cause you to scream, possibly even curse. The consequences are deafening.

Of course, it is difficult not to yell at teens when they are being so arrogant and infuriating. They won't listen to anything you say until at least the fifth time you've said it, and repetition generally leads to an increase in volume. For instance, I will stand at the bottom of the stairs and call Lulu to supper. Nothing. I'll call again, maybe a bit louder. Silence. I'll march halfway up the stairs and call her again, decidedly louder. More silence. At this point, I'll either sprint all the way up to her room, rip open her door, and demand, "Why don't you ANSWER ME?" or I will hold my position at the bottom of the stairs and shriek like a demented *maître'd*, "LULU! SUPPER!"

At this point Lulu, deeply offended, will choose from her repertoire of sassy responses: "I'm so sure you just barged in here without knocking!" or "What makes you think I'm even having dinner tonight?" or "I WAS IN THE BATHROOM! DO YOU MIND??!" And we're off to the races, while my husband has long since left the building and our family dinner is now stone cold.

Despite the fact that screaming is irresistible for some people, it makes one look awfully bad, as many folks are offended and frightened by raised voices. My proclivity for yelling may be genetic since I'm Irish, but it's also a definite liability, particularly in the South where ladies don't raise their voices, or so I've been told more than once.

Enough about me. The question here is: Why do teens yell so much?

I believe there are two different motivations. One is a "Yeah-you-better-be-scared-of-me" posturing. This bears a resemblance to the blowfish, which inflates to three times its normal size to dissuade potential enemies. Teens tend to feel attacked by any form of instruction or intrusion and often respond by yelling. For instance, if you dare to invade their bedroom to ask them to pick up their brand-new clothes from the floor, they will respond with a specific demand, as in "'Get out of my room!" or an existential cry: "Why are you trying to ruin my life?" This may feel like an attack but in reality, it's a defensive attempt to wrest back control and stake out their territory.

The other form of teen yelling is passive-aggressive, usually in response to your screaming after they've shoved you to the brink of apoplectic rage. For instance: Your son ignores your every request for help in the basement for several hours, while he creates a new profile on Facebook, text-messages forty-five friends, and locks himself in the bathroom for a disturbing length of time. Every time you climb three flights of stairs to ask him for help, you track dirt upstairs and are wasting precious time when you could be fixing the furnace. Finally, after you've dropped a wrench on your toe, torn open a blister, and sweat is pouring down your back, you march into his room and scream, "I AM NOT GOING TO ASK YOU AGAIN! GET DOWN IN THAT BASEMENT AND START HELPING THIS INSTANT!" He looks at you with narrowed eyes and yells back, "I WAS JUST COMING DOWN TO DO IT! JESUS, YOU DON'T HAVE TO SCREAM AT ME!!!" This kind of teen madness, replete with injured self-righteousness, is a dagger to the heart of any parent, as you know full well that you yelled first, you lost it, and you're a pathetic excuse for a role model. I suspect it's also deeply gratifying to teens to prove that (1) they know exactly how to get you going and

(2) you are truly an unpredictable maniac they cannot wait to be free of.

At some point, you will realize that the most effective way of dealing with your teen is to ignore his yelling. And you must do everything you can, short of gagging yourself, to prevent yourself from starting a screaming match. Yes, his behavior is appalling. That's a given. But yelling will make you feel only worse and ratchet up the emotional stakes. It's also not very effective. My mother never once raised her voice with any of the eight of us, yet she still wielded iron control over almost everything we did. And what she couldn't control, she confidently bequeathed to guilt.

A friend of mine used to exchange a holler for a whisper when she really wanted to get her teens' attention. Although I'm afraid that tactic would fall on deaf ears in my household, I find it suitably subversive and a brilliant guerrilla tactic. Yelling is old school. Catch them off guard with quiet.

Their Need to Hide
Versus Your Need to Pry

You and your teen are on a collision course to conflict and it revolves specifically around one issue: The more your teen wants to shut you out of her life, the more desperate you will become for any knowledge of what's going on behind closed doors. Specifically, the bedroom door. In the beginning of adolescence, you may find yourself wanting the door to stay open, to see the face of your child and her cute belongings and reassure yourself that she's still your child, after all.

AGONIZING EXAMPLE

This past Thanksgiving, we spent the holiday with our friends and their four teenage daughters. As everyone was getting dressed to go out to a big family dinner, the oldest daughter discovered the nice black tights she had laid out to wear had been switched to a cotton pair of less fine gauge. She was outraged and promptly accosted her sister, who screamed that of course she hadn't stolen the tights. Two other sisters quickly joined the fray, and before you could say "Happy Turkey Day," the household descended into a cacophony of accusations, shrieking, tears, door slamming, hysteria, more door slamming, and the mom's threat to ground everyone until Christmas.

At this point the dad, who works at home and is probably the most selflessly devoted, long-suffering guy I know, stepped in to enforce a ceasefire. He was met with a fusillade of bitter taunts from his girls. "How would you know what's going on? You don't know anything about us, Dad!" "You're never even here!" (When I say he works at home, I mean he is *always* home.) And my personal favorite, "You don't care about us, you just care about. . . . " (Here, the girls sort of stumbled because clearly there is nothing their dad cares about more than his daughters.) When logic failed, the girls returned to screaming at each other until finally, having driven both their parents to the point of madness, they slunk into the car and the family drove off for their blessed meal of Thanksgiving.

Personally, I was giving major thanks that for once, it wasn't my family on the warpath.

Well, she's not your baby anymore. She is her own person with her own opinions about bedroom decor, cleanliness, and accessibility, all of which can be summed up thusly: *"If you would just leave me alone and stop talking, Mom, everything would be fine! Now get out of my room!"*

These words are generally delivered with an emphatic door slam—the exclamation point at the end of a totally unacceptable outburst. This is the slam that causes you to race back in there, verbal guns blazing, when you were a mere step away from safe separation.

Lulu knew precisely how incendiary this tactic was, so she used it as frequently as possible. In fact, when we moved from our old house, the new inhabitants had to replace the entire frame of her bedroom doorway. It had been literally splintered from floor to ceiling by the repeated force of her slamming the door with all her 14-year-old might, directly in my face. Perhaps if I hadn't reacted so dramatically—never failing to threaten her with a lifetime ban on *America's Next Top Model* and the removal of every electrical gadget in her possession—she wouldn't have found repeating this scenario quite so satisfying. I constantly pledged to remove the door itself, subjecting her to a total lack of privacy and uninterrupted parental monitoring. Unfortunately, I was too unsure of my husband's ability to get the door back on its hinges to follow through. The good news is that after our move to the new house in Atlanta, she slammed the door once, I told her with no equivocation that was not going to happen in this house, and she's rarely done it again. Maybe she outgrew the need to slam, or maybe by then she realized it would only bring me into her room more quickly.

As for boys, they use their bedrooms much as the Benedictine monks use the monastery: for complete and total retreat from the world. They're also a bit like squirrels in the winter, hunkering down inside, and willing to come out only for food. If you disturb the sanctity of their rooms, they tend not to be outraged like girls; they will simply make the nest more dense and pungent to prevent further intrusions. This works remarkably well, as you are likely to be so disoriented by this microvision of what's going on in the brain of your boy, you may never venture in there again. For a good frame of reference, watch *Parenthood*, one of the all-time great movies about families. Dianne Wiest plays a single mom who is bewildered and cowed by her teenaged son. She can't bring herself to go into his padlocked room and has only the most glancing, painful conversations with him until circumstances provoke an intervention. (Warning: This kind of conflict resolution ends happily only in the movies. Don't get your hopes up and bash your way into your teen's room expecting a tearful reconciliation. You're likely to get more truth than you can handle.)

Once your 14-year-old son disappears into his room, you will not see much of him until his 18th birthday, except when you endeavor to force interaction. This may prove so unrewarding, it is often easier to stop trying. But try you must! Otherwise, your boy may become permanently monosyllabic. With my stepsons, I tried to pretend I was Anne Sullivan, devoting her life to bringing Helen Keller out of her shell. Watch the Patty Duke film to see how she contented herself with small victories like getting Helen to use utensils or splash water on her hands. When it comes to celebrating correct fork usage, I've got my party hat on!

With teen boys, it's best to forget about emotional interaction and concentrate on the physical. Your pubescent son doesn't want to feel anything. His overwhelming motivation is to shield his body from view, he is so inordinately proud, ashamed, and in awe of it. Only physical interaction

AGONIZING EXAMPLE

Cynthia was so freaked out by her son Cory's desire for privacy, she used to find every reason in the world to go into his room. Delivering laundry, glasses of water, cups of tea. Checking the batteries on the alarm clock—it was pathetic. Of course, Cory hated every intrusion and felt invaded and oversupervised. One day the two were having an argument over the multiple incursions, and Cynthia burst out crying and sobbed, "Don't you get it? I come into your room all the time because I want to see you!" Cory looked at his mom in astonishment (and pity) because that motive had never occurred to him. After that, Cynthia did try harder to stay out of Cory's room, and Cory became somewhat gentler with his request to "Please get out of my room, Mom. NOW!"

(preferably on the rough-and-tumble scale) and food (preferably huge quantities of it) will allow him to overcome his self-consciousness. As frustrating as boys can be, your heart goes out to them in their self-imposed isolation. Girls, on the other hand, will make you want to put yourself in self-imposed isolation, if only to get as far away from them as possible.

BOUNDARY VIOLATIONS

Last year I met with five senior advertising executives to discuss a major piece of business they were considering giving me. We were exploring ways we could work together even though I live in Atlanta and they work in Philadelphia. They asked me to open the video conferencing icon on my brand-new laptop to see if that might be a viable communications option. I opened the IM feature enabling the program and up popped the entire list of addresses that Lulu had thoughtfully downloaded onto my new computer. Before I could hit delete, *superabs 33*, *hotrocks*, *uloveit*, and *sweetandjuicy44* paraded across my screen like a raunchy chorus line. I looked like an Internet porn queen, which luckily in advertising only makes one "colorful." I was livid. My computer was less than forty-eight hours old and Lulu had already claimed a couple billion gigabytes as her own.

Get used to it. What's yours is theirs. But don't expect much reciprocity. (Although Lulu felt free to IM on my Mac, her own Dell is locked tighter than Fort Knox. In fact, when you try to bypass her password, the pop-up clue reads "Don't even try it, Mom.")

Teens are notorious for having porous boundaries, stealing your stuff, and invading your privacy. When I first married Larry, his 14-year-old son used to wake up every morning at 6:30 A.M., walk through our bedroom, and use our bathroom for his morning ablutions, despite the fact that he had to walk past the kids' bathroom to get into our room. After four infuriating months of this, I had to pull an Ugly Stepmother to get Larry to intervene and reassign him to the proper shower.

These encroachments into your space are utterly maddening and totally predictable. The major issue of adolescence is establishing your own identity and figuring out who you are, separate and distinct from your parents, brothers, and sisters. One way of determining your boundaries, apparently, is to push against them with all your might. Teens need to prove to themselves they exist. So they rewrite Descartes' famous words to read: *I invade your space, therefore I am.*

TALES FROM POST-TEENS • • • • • • • • •

My parent's car was an irresistible lure for me and I just figured I was entitled to use it. When I was 15, in the middle of the night I crawled out of our living room window and, at a snail's pace, slowly raised our manual garage door. And slowly pushed my mom's convertible BMW out of the driveway until it was far enough from the house to turn on the ignition without waking her. . . . Then I drove over to a guy's house so that I could make out with him. Then we drove fast out on the highway with the convertible top down, blared music, and sang our hearts out.

Once I got my license, I was allowed to drive but I was told not to smoke in the car. And I would. And my parents would smell it and I'd lie about it . . . not knowing that they could easily see I had scorched parts of the interior fabric on the ceiling of the car, something only a cigarette ash could do. It came down to a matter of respecting their property since it wasn't something I had paid for. But at that age, I'm afraid that concept didn't make much of an impression on me.

What's Logic Got to Do with It?

Teenagers are not on speaking terms with logic. Thus, when you're having an argument and cite historical fact or empirical scientific evidence, they are likely to react as if you are resorting to a cheap trick and retaliate by furiously denying the existence of things like gravity, physics, and germs. Before you've had one of these conversations, you may think other parents are exaggerating. Then you find yourself in a discussion with your teen that is so mind-bogglingly stupid, you'll want to bite off your tongue simply to stop the crazy trajectory of the conversation you're embroiled in. Biting is good; that's why God gave you teeth. Far worse is to follow your teen's twisted path of rhetoric or seek to enlighten him with the facts.

Teens don't want to know the facts and even if they did, they'd rather eat their iPods than accept the facts from you. The result? The more you try to get your teen to accept the obvious logic of your argument, the more he will resist, and you will experience an engorged fury rising up in you like Mount Vesuvius. How dare he not listen to you! What is wrong with her that she refuses to accept reason? Is your teen completely mental?

Yes. Luckily, this stage will last no more than five years, by which time you will doubt your own sanity. But I've heard the brain can regenerate itself and I'm counting on that.

Shut Up!
and Other Verbal Atrocities

There are a few words and phrases that every parent hates. In my book, it's perfectly okay to outlaw them, but that also means you can never use them yourself or your interdict will lose a lot of its oomph.

Basically, verbal atrocities can be divided into two categories: the Hugely Annoying and the Totally Outrageous. Hugely Annoying phrases include "Like I care," "As if," and "Whatever," while the Totally Outrageous classification covers all the swear words as well as blatantly defiant responses like "Shut up."

I'm campaigning hard to get "Whatever" moved into the Outrageous category because I firmly believe it's the new

AGONIZING EXAMPLE

I once had a daylong "conversation" with Lulu that began when I told her to open her windows because I had turned off the air conditioning. She was outraged that I was "so cheap" I refused to waste energy on cooling when it was a torrid 75 degrees outside. In retaliation, she informed me that opening her windows would let all the hot air in and she would not do it. Over the course of the next two hours, Lulu's room, with all its windows sealed, heated up in the direct afternoon sunlight to well over 90 degrees. I idiotically kept walking in to urge her to open her windows. She refused. The argument ended with my trying to force her to read the encyclopedia to prove that shutting your windows on a hot day creates an oven-like "greenhouse effect." Naturally she remained completely unconvinced and was happy to swelter to prove her point.

"F.U." When your kid says "What-e-ver" to you, she actually means "I couldn't care less what you're flapping your lips about and I don't agree with anything you say, but I can't be bothered to even respond because that is so totally beneath me, and p.s. F.U." Whenever somebody says "Whatever" to me, I'm sorely tempted to respond "Yeah, F.U., too," which isn't me at my articulate best. And that's why "Whatever" is verboten in our household.

The less egregious but thoroughly annoying "It's all good" is the passive-aggressive stoner credo that similarly sets my teeth on edge. This is one of my stepdaughter's favorites, usually used to point out that I'm getting worked up over something totally inconsequential, like a severed sewer main or a 700 percent increase in her college tuition. The subtext of "It's all good" is that there is no point in getting upset about something you can't change, so you might as well roll with it and stay cool because it will all work out in the end. (Inhale mind-altering substance here.)

While I remember with a great deal of fondness having those exact sentiments when I was young and stoned, now that I'm old, stone-cold sober, and trying to run a household, I find it infuriating. "It's all good" is one of those life philosophies beloved by college freshmen that are destined to be slapped out of one's skull with a good global reality check. For starters, everything is *not* all good. Is Darfur all good? Is global warming all good? Is artificial creamer all good? I think not.

Likewise, teens adore the Totally Outrageous category of retorts because using one is like tossing a grenade into a polka hall. "Shut up" leads the pack of disrespectful adages, followed by all the swears you can think of: "Fuck you," "Asshole," "You suck," "You're such a bitch," "Dickhead," and so on. Obviously, your teen should never be allowed to say any of these things to you. But since teens hear stuff like this daily on cable, the radio, and the Internet, as well as in the halls of Congress (thanks, Dick Cheney), chances are very good that somewhere along the line, you'll be confronted with a curse or two.

How should you respond? I'm in a precarious pulpit here since I spent my formative years in advertising (the potty-mouth boot camp of careers) and I am on a first-name basis with most curse words, as anyone who knows me can verify. Obviously, my strictures against swearing carry very little weight. Yet my kids rarely swear, perhaps due to the fact that they want to be as little like me as possible.

I've found that the only viable response to a frontal swear attack is to say as quietly as possible, "You are not allowed to use that language in this house." Then beat a hasty retreat.

Tales From Post-Teens ● ● ● ● ● ● ● ●

One day I was arguing with my mom, and that usually
didn't end well. I could never keep my big mouth shut and
always said something I shouldn't. I believe I gave her the
usual teenage reply: "I can do whatever I want!" To which
she responded by grabbing me by the arm, dragging me to
the front door, and depositing me on the front porch. This
was accompanied by her saying, "Well, if you think you
can do anything, then you can find your own place to
live." Obviously, I had nowhere to go, so after about five
minutes of standing on the porch, I knocked on the door
and asked if I could come home. I'm pretty sure I was
grounded then for my fresh mouth.

The retreat part is essential as the normal teen response to
your quiet, firm directive is bound to be "Fuck off." If you
don't "hear" that, you've made your point.

You can't ban most words, but if you pick and choose carefully, you may be able to outlaw the ones that make your
blood boil. And that's worth the effort, in my humble opinion.

5

OH, THE SNEAKY, UNDERHANDED THINGS THEY'LL DO

IT'S NOT YOUR IMAGINATION. YOUR TEENAGER HAS lost his or her mind. Or more specifically, he simply hasn't gotten around to using most of it yet.

Not to worry—it's developmental. My sister (the one with a medical degree) told me that brain scans reveal very few signs of activity in the frontal lobe of adolescents' brains. Apparently, it doesn't fully mature until one's early 20s. The underdeveloped area is called the dorsal lateral prefrontal cortex and it plays a critical role in decision making; in establishing values, conscience, and a moral code; and in understanding the future consequences of actions. For instance, if you are text-messaging while driving seventy-five miles per hour down the freeway, you're a tad more likely to wrap yourself around a telephone pole than if you kept your eyes on the road. Useful stuff like that. Yet as far as I can tell, the only thing most teenagers use their frontal lobes for is deciding whether to super-size their meal.

In the interim, *you* must be their brain. My sister explained that one therapeutic approach posits if teenagers' brains aren't mature enough to function properly, parents must act as their external frontal lobes, frequently reminding teens of consequences and right versus wrong. (Of course, teenagers' listening and appreciation lobes are apparently also undeveloped, meaning you're going to get nothing but crap for acting as their conscience and values coach.)

Sure, teens have soft-serve brains *and* they're totally immature *and* they have no idea what they're doing half the time. That still doesn't mean teenagers don't fully believe in their own bullshit—specifically, that they are 100 million percent smarter than you. And would do a far better job running the world if only somebody would put them in charge (while continuing to pay their bills and put away their laundry). It's this last bit of icing on the Cake of Teen Condescension that makes you long to clobber them.

I was a passenger in the car while a friend of mine was giving his daughter driving lessons and listened to this priceless exchange:

"Claire, you have to keep both hands on the wheel if you want to pass your driver's test. It's the only safe way to drive."

"You have no idea what you're talking about, Dad! I have much more control when I have just one hand on the wheel. And then I can spin the wheel around with the heel of my hand without ruining my nails. See?"

Naturally, the car careened straight into the oncoming lane, which was blessedly empty.

In times like these, instead of launching into a blistering lecture, simply give teens the abbreviated advice their own brains should be manufacturing, particularly in the realm of making good choices. Then envision a future when their lobes have finally leaped into action and you'll have been proven right about almost everything.

Lying, Sneaking, and Misbehaving: The Teen Trifecta

In every conversation I've had with former teenagers, one thing was perfectly clear. They lied. A lot. They snuck around behind their parents' backs. And they did some incredibly imbecilic, self-destructive, and dangerous stuff. These are kids who are now responsible, successful young adults. But a couple years ago, they still acted like—teenagers.

For some reason, this is incredibly comforting to me. It offers me hope and lets me know that I am not alone. It also makes me deeply resent the books that caution you to never undermine your teen's fragile self-esteem with criticism or confrontation. Or far worse, to trust them implicitly and have friendly little talks with them, offering them positive encouragement and constructive ideas they will gratefully embrace and put into action. What a load of crap! If there is one thing that is perfectly clear from my research, it is that teens mostly behave abominably towards their parents. They make bad choices, are staggeringly unappreciative, mouth off, and challenge authority until their parents totally lose it. And then they grow up to become wonderful young adults who wonder why they were such awful creeps to the people who love them the most.

But just so you know: At this point of adolescence, even the best teens are pretty gnarly. And it all begins with sex, drugs, and booze.

TALES FROM POST-TEENS • • • • • • • • •

While spending the night at a friend's house when I was 14, I snuck out after everybody was asleep and walked over to the house of a boy whose parents were out of town. We decided to see a girlfriend of mine, Katie, whose parents were super-strict and would not let her leave the house. (Well, it WAS 3 A.M.) In addition, she lived almost five miles away, so I convinced Adam that I was a very good driver and got him to give me the keys to his mom's station wagon to drive over to pick up Katie. We climbed up a tree near her bedroom, crawled across the roof of the garage, got her out of her bedroom, and stayed up all night driving around.

❧

The dumbest thing my parents said to me in high school was "I trust you" and then left my brothers and me home alone . . . how totally lame. I don't think I even need to tell you how that story ended . . . with a big crazy party and a whole bunch of drunk kids.

❧

Growing up, I was studious, quiet, incredibly dorky, and pretty much a loner. I wasn't a bad girl by any stretch. But I did lie (to get out of trouble) and snuck around behind my parents' back (to avoid getting in trouble). Oh, and I was sort of a kleptomaniac for a while. . . .

Sex: To Have or Not to Have?
(It's Not Your Question)

Few things strike more terror into the parental heart than the issue of sex. First, there's the possibility of pregnancy and the thrill of full-time grandparenthood when parenthood itself is making you ill. Then, there are AIDS, HPV, and other STDs as potential side effects. It's so unfair that you can't just tie their knees together and be done with it!

As a parent, you know that having sex as a young teen is a bad idea, but good luck promoting that. Boys are obsessed with sex and consider virginity a scourge that is probably emblazoned on their foreheads—*Hasn't Done It Yet!* Their sole motivation seems to be to shed their virtue as quickly as possible. At the same time, boys are perplexed by and terrified of their own bodies, much less the curvy, fragrant, and foreign bodies of the girls they're presumably trying to seduce. Boys' hearts can also get broken quite easily, so the last thing they need to be doing is getting more emotionally attached. And there is the completely unforeseen (to them) possibility that they will get a girl pregnant, she will make a unilateral decision to have the baby, and they will become fathers with absolutely no choice in the matter. (This recently happened to a friend's son and now this college junior has a child with a woman he spent exactly one fateful night with, and is looking at eighteen years of child support.)

Girls, because they can get pregnant, seem ten times more vulnerable than boys but that isn't necessarily true. One thing is certain, though: A girl's reputation can be scarred by her sexual choices in a way a boy's never will be. The world will slap "cheap," "slutty," and "sleazy" labels on a promiscuous girl, while the same behavior in a boy earns the "stud" and "player" tags. The most valuable thing you can offer your

WORDS OF WISDOM

Janet's daughter Cassie is a bright and accomplished junior in high school with a longtime boyfriend. Cassie is deeply in love with this boy, who is also a very good kid. The couple recently decided to have sex and Cassie asked her mom to take her to the doctor for birth control pills. After a long talk with both teens about having sex and all the consequences of that decision, Janet agreed to get Cassie on birth control, but she is not allowing this to be a gauzy, romantic moment. She's been clinically honest with Cassie about penetration, yeast infections, oral and anal sex, lubrication, and other fun topics. And she regularly has conversations with the boyfriend about Cassie's menstrual cycle, her propensity to spot when she forgets to take her pill, and his need to have a backup plan if he is going to ejaculate inside her daughter's womb. As far as I can tell, Janet's willingness to talk frankly about all the ins and outs of sex is acting like a fire hose of cold water on any incipient desire.

daughter is not a diatribe about the unfairness of it (although that's well worth mentioning) but an awareness that it's true.

When I begin to get freaked out on the subject, I try to pretend that I'm Swedish, since Scandinavians appear to be utterly relaxed and nonjudgmental about teens having sex. Their kids fornicate like bunny rabbits, yet don't seem any more screwed up than our teens. Maybe the American obsession with sex is actually preventing us from being able to see it as a natural part of life rather than an enormous, looming threat. Unfortunately, I'm not Scandinavian, I'm Irish Catholic

and hardwired to associate sex with guilt and horrible consequences. But some of my friends are a lot more creative than I
am—Janet among them.

When it comes to sex, I'm all about procrastination. I believe the longer you wait to have it, the better are the odds
you'll be able to handle it. Or, as Rosie O'Donnell was memo-
rably quoted, "Nobody looks back and thinks gee, I wish I
would have had sex sooner." (Unless it's a guy, who usually
wishes he could have figured out a way to have sex *in utero*.)
Delaying tactics are what it's all about.

A friend of mine said that her son and daughter seemed to
respond to the message that you don't want to steal anything
from the future by experiencing sex too early. "You've got to
save some fun, exciting stuff for college" was her promotional
pitch, which seemed to resonate with her teens. Another
friend shared that her daughter didn't trust guys not to dine
and dash, so to speak. Although the mom didn't want to
man-bash, she did nothing to dissuade her daughter from
that opinion and was secretly thrilled when her daughter
started dating a guy who expressed his commitment to absti-
nence on his Facebook page. My personal experience with
Lulu has been a shuddering cold shoulder any time I try to
bring up the topic of sex, but I'm still trying to have "The
Talk" any time the subject comes up. And of course the HPV
vaccine gives every mother a good chance to discuss sexual
activity and the many rewards of waiting.

SEX AND EMOTIONAL ATTACHMENTS

Looking back to the Pleistocene period when I was free to sleep
around, I would say the danger of getting emotionally attached
to someone totally inappropriate is exponentially increased

Tales From Post Teens ● ● ● ● ● ● ● ● ●

My mom was always asking me if I was having sex with my high school boyfriends—in fact, she was obsessed about it. So I was really mad when I found out she walked in on my eighth-grade brother getting a blowjob in our den, and she just quietly backed out and never said a word. I couldn't believe the double standard, although I guess that's pretty typical.

when you're having sex, as opposed to merely dating. (And that includes oral sex and "friends with benefits.") I honestly believe it's not in most teenagers' emotional repertoire to deal with the weight and heft of a sexual relationship. But assuming teens will have sex and will get attached, what happens next?

First, continue to preach to your boys and girls the need for birth control and the critical importance of practicing safe sex. Don't be one of those words-only wonks; enable them to get access to the products they need. You are far too young and cute to be a grandparent, and it goes without saying that your teens aren't ready to raise anything more than a beer can.

Yet the deeper implications of teen sex go far beyond the physical gymnastics. Boys tend to be so grateful that they are being allowed access to the golden triangle, they'll do almost anything to guarantee that nothing interferes, which can lead to obsessive relationships and brain-dead behavior. All the blood rushing to their engorged members robs their brains of life-giving oxygen, or some similar medical explanation. For girls, the idea that someone openly wants, desires, and chooses them offers a life raft on the ocean of insecurity that is adolescence. Both impulses infuse the sexual relationship

TALES FROM POST-TEENS ● ● ● ● ● ● ● ●

In my house, my parents were quite good at making their presence known prior to entering a room if one of us was there with someone of the opposite sex. That's a habit I highly recommend for all parents. Sure, your kids will roll their eyes and act like it is totally lame, but deep down they really appreciate it. And it ends up avoiding uncomfortable situations for everybody involved. I found out the hard way that other parents weren't always so cautious. . . .

I was spending Thanksgiving Day at my boyfriend's house and we had been hanging out in his room before dinner, and like dumb teenagers, we were fooling around. His dad came up to tell us it was time for dinner and didn't knock. He walked in to find me with my shirt completely off, boobs half-exposed—it was very embarrassing, especially since we made direct eye contact. Needless to say, he walked out without saying a word. But then I had to go down and have Thanksgiving dinner with the whole family. Honestly, I don't know who was more embarrassed, me or his dad.

with far greater importance than is warranted by the fleeting shelf life of the typical high school romance.

Having said that, I remember full well how passionate, gripping, and dramatic high school liaisons can be. That's precisely why I believe parents should constantly remind teens that these relationships are undependable, mercurial, and for practice only—a good way to learn about yourself, but nothing that is supposed to last. This is not to say parents shouldn't take their teenager's *emotions* seriously; it's to suggest that they don't need to take the *relationship* too seriously. A dispassionate parental stance offers a critical counterbalance to the whacked-out emotions teens invest in their romantic lives.

Yet many parents seem to feel that to stay "connected" to their teens they must take these romances seriously and actually promote them. In effect, this amounts to communicating that the relationship is essential and will last if enough energy is pumped into it. Don't go there. Take a page from your own dad's book and protect your teen with a studied indifference (if not open hostility) to the romance.

SEX AND COMING OUT

Lest you forget, high school is a veritable merry-go-round of humiliation, shame, guilt, and self-consciousness. And that's on a good day. Teenage life can only be twice as harrowing if you're gay or lesbian. Or is that old chestnut even valid in this new day and age? Obviously, a lot depends on how progressive and open-minded your teen's school and community are. I don't have any personal experience with this myself, so I'll share a few stories from friends.

❧

When Sam was 12, he was a cuddly, angelic-looking kid with a passionate love for theater and art. It never occurred to his dad that he might be gay, but his mother Carol knew from the time he was 2. By the time Sam was 16, he had long black spiked hair and was in full goth mode, typically wearing more eyeliner and mascara than Cher, a long black trench coat, knee-high biker boots, black pantaloons, and fishnet stockings. He looked like Alan Cumming in *Cabaret*—not exactly a closet case.

⁣⁣⁣⁣⁣⁣ ✎

Carol's biggest worry with Sam being gay was the fear that he would be shunned and mocked in school. She cried her eyes out anticipating that cruel rejection. As it happened, her fears were groundless as Sam was exuberantly gay and his sexual orientation seemed to only make him more well-liked in school. He was voted Most Popular, was the center of all high school activities and plays, and never seemed to suffer from feeling like an outsider. What Carol did have to worry about was Sam's older brother Aron, who was a varsity football player, terminally heterosexual, and not at all pleased about living with his Barbie-loving, cross-dressing baby brother. Aron loved Sam a lot, but he didn't always like living with him. Carol was always bending over backward to be sure that Sam felt as if he could express who he was, but what she didn't realize was how difficult it would be to also respect the rights of Aron, who didn't have any desire to live in a flamboyantly gay household.

⁣⁣⁣⁣⁣⁣ ✎

Juggling teens of different sexual orientation has got to be tough. But at least it's out in the open. When I asked one of my closest friends, Stephen, who is 40, when he'd known he was gay, he replied, "Pretty much always." When I asked Stephen when he'd come out to his parents, he said, "Never." Despite his warm and close relationship with his parents, his sexuality is permanently off the record. Stephen is in a committed long-term relationship that is better than most mar-

TALES FROM POST TEENS ● ● ● ● ● ● ● ●

I first suspected I was gay in eighth grade, when I had a crush on my riding teacher. That crush was all-consuming, and afforded me the opportunity to experience plenty of teenage angst. The thought of mentioning it to my parents was horrifying, really, even though I knew they would be accepting of my sexuality. I was more worried about my peers and whether I was doomed to be an outsider forever.

A month after I left home for college, I fell in love with a woman and came out to my parents over the phone. They were extremely supportive—almost *too* supportive. My mom said she'd always known and asked why hadn't I told her earlier. She seemed excited, like having a gay daughter was something to brag about. I even got sort of angry at her, because I was extremely eager to defend my privacy.

My advice to parents of gay teens would be to broadcast their love and support always, but not to pry or push. I think if my mom had been slightly less excited about my sexuality and more respectful of my privacy, I would have come out to her earlier.

riages I know of, yet his domestic life with his partner is unacknowledged by his parents, even as they visit the couple at home. That seems heartbreaking—and pointless—to me.

But today is a new day. And our teens—bless their everloving, straight-or-gay obnoxious hearts—are not about to push their sexuality under the carpet, or let their parents live in a fantasyland of happily-ever-after. Damn it!

Bad Friends

Not long ago, I read a study that claimed once children reach the age of 12, friends have a far greater impact on their decisions, values, and activities than parents. Well, duhhhhhh. The time teens spend with you, the intolerable, boring people who brought them into this world, is a minuscule blip compared to the hours piled on hours they devote to examining every facet of their friends' fascinating thoughts and feelings. Thus, it's worth discussing how you can influence your child's choice of friends.

Basically, you don't have a whole lot of weight here.

In the ninth grade, my friend Angela went off the deep end under the influence of a wild, thoroughly self-destructive friend. I think because this girl was from a "good family," Angela's parents didn't intervene. That was how life was back in the day; parents had a lot of rules about the big stuff but they didn't micromanage. In Angela's case, however, they probably should have: This friend of hers was a terrible influence, casting a despotic spell that shook Angela right off the straight and narrow path of athletics and achievement. Angela started doing drugs, abandoned her other friends, and began to lose confidence and see herself as an underachieving outsider. In fact, Angela never fully recovered from that wrong turn, and still wonders what she might have accomplished if she hadn't followed her friend into rebellion.

What can you do when your kids start hanging out with friends who are smoking, drinking, doing drugs, and/or generally leading them over the edge? (Or what do you do when your kid, God forbid, *is* the bad influence?)

It is possible to move schools—when they're in middle school. I yanked Lulu out of public school after sixth grade when a posse of boys started calling the house at midnight, raving about her 12-year-old booty, dropping the F-bomb, and offering to sell me drugs. By the time high school rolls around, however, you probably won't be able to pry kids out of their school with a crowbar (unless it's their idea). You'd have better luck sending them to boot camp. If you distrust or fear one of your child's friends, talk to the guidance counselor at school (the keeper of all teen knowledge) and see if you have cause for concern. It is certainly okay to refuse to have that kid over to your home and to not allow your kid to go over to the offensive kid's house, a course of action I highly recommend. You may not have much control over what goes on in the schoolyard but you are the queen (or king) of all time before and after school. Some parents seem to feel they have to be Politically Correct and not discriminate against any young delinquent. I believe you have to be Parentally Correct and discriminate like crazy. Talk to your teens about their friendships and relationships in a calm, nonthreatening manner without overtly bashing their friends, but don't expect any kind of positive response to the conversation. It's likely to be as welcomed as the Grand Inquisition.

Sadly, our jurisdiction over the amount of contact teens have with their friends has been mightily compromised by the Internet and cell phone, which easily allow kids to communicate sans parental monitoring. This brave new wireless world we're living in can be intimidating, and quite frankly, it can seem like we don't have the authority we once did. Steve Jobs has it. However, my advice is to fake it. You still have the right and the means to get them off the phone, unplug them from the Internet, and check their cell phone calls (although who in their right mind is going to wade through the 400-page monthly phone bill?). Miraculously, your kids will probably buy into this power structure, no matter how ephemeral, because they're hardwired to believe you are in control and out to ruin all their fun. By all means, make rules about how and when they can use their cell phones and computer, and be aware of their choice of friends. You haven't done all that heavy groundwork just to let some little schmuck swagger in and undermine it all.

MIND- AND LIFE-ALTERING SUBSTANCES

If you suspect your teen is smoking pot, snorting cocaine, or popping pills, you can start drug-testing him and withhold privileges like driving until he shapes up. Driving is the ultimate privilege in a teen's life, so don't hesitate to use it as a carrot. Or a stick. But once you've taken away the car or the license, what else do you have to bargain with? Almost nothing.

Pot smoking, delightful as we once found it, is not the harmless pursuit of happiness that we once believed in college. Sad to say, but today's pot is stronger than ever and it does tend to inhibit, if not entirely wipe out, a teenager's dubious motivation. My best friend's son smoked his way through high school and half of college. Looking back, he'll admit it's probably the sole reason he quit tennis, eventually flunked out of college, had lame relationships, and took five and a half years to graduate with a major he didn't even like. At 25, he's paid a big price for his stoner ways, had to retake a lot of courses (at his own expense), and wasted a boatload of time. Now he gets high on stretching and playing basketball, which wastes an equal amount of time, but at least he can think clearly—and God knows, he's limber.

Then, of course, there's the heavy hitter in the room. That would be alcohol—most adults' drug of choice and the socially acceptable way to get jacked up at every possible occasion. Alcohol is so easy to acquire, it's not unusual for kids to start drinking in ninth grade. In fact, you should expect that your kids will have exposure to booze, as well as the opportunity to imbibe at that age.

Therefore, it's imperative you send them out into the world armed with education about drinking, drugs, and powers of resistance. Schools do a fairly good job educating teens about the influence of drugs and alcohol, but the role-playing is up to you. It's not enough to urge them to say no when pressured to imbibe: They need to practice exactly what they're going to say. If you manage to make it a game, with creativity and conviction rewarded, you can dispense some of the awkwardness of this exercise. One Asian girl I know tells people she is allergic to alcohol, then goes on to explain that about 50 percent of Chinese, Japanese, and Korean people have an impaired ability to break down alcohol and will suffer a severe flushing reaction if they drink (true!). Another teen tells people his pancreas once failed and now he cannot process alcohol at all. The important thing is for your child to have a position he or she is comfortable and familiar with, because the pressure to capitulate will be there. (Of course, let's not forget that some teens have no desire to resist experimentation.)

The idea is to hold the parental line on the fact that under-age drinking or drug use is dangerous, illegal, forbidden, and has consequences. And thus, your children are *not* allowed to do it. If you consistently message this, you won't liquor-proof your children's future, but you will help them be smarter about it and communicate that you aren't winking at the transgression—which the law certainly won't. (In fact, the legal system is more hard-line on teen drinking than ever; one kid I know was arrested at 18 for drinking and *walking* in our little town; another 25-year-old got a DUI for drinking and mopeding.) Nor should you be capitulating to popular opinion, like some parents who serve alcohol in their homes so "at least we'll know where the kids are and can keep them safe." Safely soused, that is. Serving alcohol to minors in your home is also illegal and carries with it a hefty fine in some states, just so you know.

Since the dawn of time, kids have been drinking and sneaking around. So make sure you know where your teens are when they go out, and that adults are in attendance at parties, sleepovers, and so on. Check up on them routinely and frequently. Be a big, fat party-pooper. Then be realistic with yourself. Accept the possibility that, at some point in high school, your teen may experiment with alcohol and/or drugs and hopefully get sicker than a dog, throw up all night, and feel bathed in remorse come morning. I've included a raft of stories from young adults whose exploits should assure you that if your teens are up to no good, at least you're not alone. Hopefully they too will grow out of their bad habits and into an adulthood that is so action-packed and demanding, there's precious little time to get hammered and hung over. Ah, maturity!

TALES FROM POST-TEENS ● ● ● ● ● ● ● ●

One weekend when my parents stupidly went away and left me and my older sister Kaitlin at home alone, we threw a party and all got drunk. I was still pretty young (15 or so), and I ended up totally hammered on gin for the first time. I couldn't function, so when Kaitlin and her friends wanted to go get something to eat, they decided to drop me and my one other very drunk friend off at another friend's house. The catch was that no one was home at this friend's house; the whole family was out of town. We broke in and hung out 'til Kaitlin came back to pick us up. In that time, I barfed in the house, my friend burned a piece of furniture, and we let the cat out of its crate and it peed all over the place. Needless to say, the people knew we'd been there and we got in a lot of trouble. The good news is I have not drunk gin since then, can't even get a whiff of it without feeling queasy. I smelled like a pine tree for days.

RESPECTING THEIR PRIVACY
(AND OTHER OVERRATED VIRTUES)

How are you ever going to know if your teens are having sex, drinking, smoking pot, or lying if you don't do a little sleuthing? You're not. So it makes all the sense in the world to see if they're going where they said and doing what they claimed. Occasionally poke through their stuff. And make sure they realize they are not yet adults with full adult privileges and so they will be under random surveillance. Your ignorance is their bliss, and that is not a good thing.

Of course, your teen will treat every incursion into his or her stuff as a complete outrage, possibly prosecutable, and act as if you've committed a constitutional assault on the Teen Bill of Rights. Big whup. They'll get over it. From time immemorial, parents have gone through their kids' drawers, pockets, and closets. Yet today if you mention that you're a snoop, some parent is going to look at you as if you're J. Edgar Hoover on a bender. I'm amazed at the resistance some parents apparently feel about invading Junior's personal space. No offense, but that sounds like a parent who is so deep in denial, she still trusts her child to tell Mommy everything. Read the above teen stories before you take that to the bank, folks.

In my humble opinion, it's not very wise to totally respect your teen's privacy. I've heard the philosophy that kids will rise to the trust placed in them. Again, consult the previous stories—all written by kids who were veritable paragons of virtue on paper. Now, I'm keenly aware that, when you invade your teen's space and stuff, you are not being completely trustworthy yourself. So what? You're the parent. Besides, it counts as dishonesty only if you've specifically promised your teen you won't pry. (Wuss!) In fact, one could argue that it's your parental responsibility to be aware of what your child is doing and if you're purposefully turning a blind eye to the evidence before you, it's an abdication of that charge.

I do draw the line at reading a teen's journal, though. Then you're invading your child's thoughts and feelings, not monitoring her actions, and there is a difference. I consider journals to be sacred ground and I'm so hoping to encourage writing, I'd do anything to make it a safe, inviolable space. I admit I did read my sister's journals once or twice when we were growing up and it made me feel awful. I couldn't bear doing it again.

AGONIZING EXAMPLE

One of my favorite trite tips from books on teens is this gem: "The more you trust your teen, the more trustworthy he or she will become."

Simplistic statements like these drive me crazy because they create the expectation that if you do A, your teenager will do B. The one predictable thing about teenagers is that they will *not* respond to you in a logical, rational, or productive manner. They will demand to be trusted, then steal your car. They will insist upon handling their own homework, then forget to do a term paper. They will hide their emotions and feelings, then complain that you don't know who they are. There is nothing simple about raising a teen; in fact, it's about as complex a personal relationship as exists. Expect *that*.

One last caveat: There is a continuum of letting go that makes it okay to invade the privacy of a 14-year-old but sort of pathetic to be doing it when the kid is 18. As with most everything else, you'll have to stagger through this privacy dilemma by Braille, feeling your way through the maze. Just don't get suckered into the "trust me" pit. It's bottomless.

6

COPING
MECHANISMS

TEENAGERS LOVE TO PISS OFF THEIR PARENTS. SERI-
ously, they love it. They live for the moments when they
manage to combine precisely the right elements of insolence
and defiance and can witness your face flush, your nostrils
flare, and your hands tremble with the urge to choke the living sass right out of them. As you have no doubt witnessed
by now, teens will challenge you over issues large and small,
and argue about stuff so petty you can't imagine how they
work up the energy. Despite the fact that turning off a light
presents a seemingly insurmountable hurdle, arguing with
you for four hours about the length of time they are permit-
ted to lollygag in the shower poses no similar challenge.
They're totally up for that kind of pointless debate.

Knowing that conflict is your teen's *goal* may prevent you
from doing something idiotic, like engaging in a showdown

simply because you're right. The fact that you are right is of very little consequence when the end result is a big altercation that will leave you feeling drained and enraged. The more you try to go head to head with your teenager, the more resistance you are likely to meet. And the angrier you are going to feel. Glancing encounters that don't belabor your point are going to preserve a lot more of your emotional equilibrium.

In this chapter, we'll examine some ways to avoid the inferno.

THREATS AND THE THREATENING THREATENERS WHO USE THEM

"If you use that tone of voice with me once more, I swear to God you are not going to the prom."

"I am two seconds away from throwing your iPod out the god-damn window, mister."

"That's it. You're grounded for the rest of the summer."

What makes parents say stuff like this? We know we're not going to toss out the iPod. (It costs $300 and is designed to break in thirteen months anyhow.) We're not going to cause them to miss their prom (even though our own was instantly forgettable and/or regrettable). And who could bear the horror of having them around the house every minute of the summer? Yet somehow, making threats we're never going to enforce is irresistible to all but the most enlightened parents.

For one thing, threats give us the illusion of power. We feel like we're putting our foot down, when it's actually the teenager who is getting a leg up, since he knows full well we're not going to follow through. Threats carry the illusion of justice being meted out, as we imagine our children suffering a catastrophic eclipsing of their social lives without the guilt of having to make that happen. Threats are the prod we employ to try to jolt our mulish children into some semblance of action.

But in reality, threats are tactics that imply you're on the defensive. If the threat is something you're willing to enforce, fine. It must be quick, easy to deploy, and a fair and logical consequence for disobedience or lack of responsibility. (*Pick up your room or you're not going out tonight.*) It should not be something long-term or you'll forget to enforce it and your child will forget why he's being punished. The more grandiose the punishment, the better the threat will make you feel—and the less likely you are to make it stick.

The problem with serial, addicted threateners like me is that our threats become more and more wildly random and irrational, until they lose all meaning. Your teen, knowing your tenuous grasp on sanity, will goad you into a ridiculous, escalating pyramid of promised punishments just for the hell of it. A particularly clever device my kids have used is the "Go ahead" response, which sends the entire conversation into hyperspace. It's hard to be levelheaded and think about what you're saying when you're hopping mad. Far better to "threaten" something that will solve the problem, rather than blurting out something punitive that, when you calm down, you won't want to inflict. That only makes you look dumb and weak . . . and you'll have plenty of opportunity to feel that way as it is.

THE TRUTH ABOUT CONSEQUENCES

When Lulu was 8 and I had the prescience to realize I was already in deep parenting doo-doo, I went to a seminar in which we were advised to allow our kids to suffer the natural consequences of their actions. A couple examples were to let them go hungry if they didn't eat their food and become very cold if they refused to wear their mittens. I totally got that

AGONIZING EXAMPLE

A. PATH OF MAXIMUM AGONY

"If I get one more notice that your homework isn't done, I'm going to take away your iPod."

"Go ahead."

"I will, don't you worry. And maybe I'll cancel your cell phone, too."

"Who cares?"

"Oh yeah? Then I might as well cancel our cable as well."

"So what?"

"Fine. Then I'll cancel your cell phone and cable—and I'm taking away your computer, too."

"Go ahead."

At this point, you've completely decimated your credibility because you're taking away the very thing he needs to do his stupid homework. And he knows it.

B. NEW AND IMPROVED AGONY

"If I get one more notice that your math homework isn't done, I'm hiring a tutor and you'll work with him three times a week."

"Go ahead."

"Good, then we're clear."

concept, although I'm enough of a control freak and worry-wart that I wasn't able to apply it very frequently. I opted for the dining table showdown, which involved sitting for hours waiting for Lulu to "try" her fish sticks. Or running after the school bus, climbing aboard, and forcing her chubby blue digits into some mittens.

I have another fatal flaw that inhibits my full embracing of natural consequences: the closely held belief that I am the parent and my kids "should" do what I say. As the kids have gotten older, this belief has become a liability of epic proportions as my self-appointed position as the Final Authority becomes more irrelevant and progressively more untrue. Your parental task is to gradually remove yourself from the responsibility platform and allow your teen to figure out what she should or shouldn't do.

The problem, of course, with allowing your teen to suffer natural consequences is that the stakes get a lot higher. Instead of his cute little hands getting blue with cold, he "forgets" to study for the SAT and gets an 850. Instead of her tummy rumbling with hunger, she develops a serious eating disorder. It's difficult to maintain your equanimity when the natural consequences can change your teen's life or impact what's possible for the future.

Dyed-in-the-wool interventionists will insist that they are only protecting their child's best interests. But let's face it, we live in a world of Boomer parents far too invested in their children's future to sit on the sidelines and watch that investment founder. When parents all around you are rushing in to save their teen from getting cut from the school play or propping up a mediocre athlete with professional training, it's hard to hold on to the idea that your kid should get by on her own merits or be his own best friend. Much less suffer consequences that you could easily deflect with a flurry of phone calls and favors called in.

The truth is, the game has changed. Natural consequences are as outdated as the IBM Selectric and in allowing them to happen to your child, you're likely to have a lonely time of it. However, your teen might be a lot better off for your discipline. While it's mighty hard to be the only parents on the block who aren't rushing in to rescue their teen, the sense of independence and character that is learned by screwing something up royally and having to fix it all by yourself is worth its weight in gold.

When I was 16, I rammed my dad's car directly into a parked car, causing $2,000 worth of damage. To pay that back, I had to work as a waitress for two years, serving scrapple, shoofly pie, and apple fritter sundaes at an ersatz Pennsylvania Dutch restaurant every weekend, starting at 6 A.M. I didn't feel mad about it; or if I did, I was too tired to mouth off. My parents didn't feel sorry for me and they weren't grateful that I repaid the debt. It was expected. But if Lulu wrecked my car, I'm sure my first instinct would be to buy a replacement within a month and never presume to interrupt her study, sports, and social schedule to ask her to fit in a measly job. (I hope I'm wrong about this.)

That's my truth about consequences. It's a great concept, but hard as hell to implement when you've spent a lifetime bending over backward to prevent your child from experiencing them. If you start small, gradually allowing your child to make choices and not intervening as the situation plays out, you may begin to see the wisdom of the process. Your child may grow in confidence, owning his own choices and knowing he can survive a bad decision as well as a good one. And you won't have to feel responsible for managing every single aspect of your teenager's life, which will be a giant weight off your aching shoulders.

THE TAKE-AWAY ON TAKING STUFF AWAY

The great thing about teenagers these days is they have so much stuff, it's a veritable smorgasbord of things you can take

TALES FROM POST-TEENS ● ● ● ● ● ● ● ●

I grew up in a relatively wealthy household, but I had to work and pay for everything myself (obviously, not food or shelter, but my car, my insurance, and anything "extra"). Every other kid on the block got a shiny new BMW or similar car for their 16th birthday. My brother and I scraped together our savings for an '89 Accord. The other kids had weekly nail appointments and designer clothes, but my mom taught us how to bargain-shop at TJ Maxx. Other kids bossed their parents around and demanded rides, money, and parties. My brother and I asked nicely and were often told no.

At the time, it was "totally unfair" and "the end of my life." Now? Those other kids are still living at home (or in penthouses that their parents pay for). They're helpless and lazy and at some point, they're going to be faced with some sort of reality check—something, I've found, that is way better to be introduced to at an early age. My parents taught me about hard work and its rewards. Sure, they got us out of scrapes every now and again. But they didn't fight our battles for us.

All of my friends "had their parents take care of" whatever was needed. My parents showed us how to take care of it ourselves. At 15, it's embarrassing to have to work and not have everything given to you. But at 28, still having your parents "take care of everything" is even more pathetic, for sure.

away. Cell phones. iPods. Nintendo. CDs. DVDs. Xbox. iPhones. Cars. Trucks. Vespas. Oh my.

But be forewarned: Teens are so attached to their devices they are likely to perceive their removal as a genuine amputation and/or assault and battery. And then there's the problem of the return of the vital objects. Taking away a teen's toys is somewhat akin to yanking all your money out of the stock market when the Dow tanks, as savvy investors like myself are wont to do. At first, you feel proactive and vindicated. The only problem is: How do you know when to put your money back in? (My trick is to sell low, buy high.) Likewise, when your teen has committed some lunatic atrocity and you've taken away his favorite electronic device, how do you know what constitutes a sufficient period of deprivation? Too brief a loss (I once removed and returned Lulu's cell phone three times in less than ten minutes) and you look like the weenie parent you deeply suspect you are. Too long and they may forget you have it, which sort of undercuts the power of the reprobation. It's a delicate balance.

Much like the issue of making threats, taking stuff away from teenagers is best handled without anger. And optimally, when they aren't there. A fight avoided is a fight won. Lest we forget, our teens now likely exceed our size and if sufficiently challenged or enraged, they are likely to try to physically prevent us from taking away their beloved things. That's not a place you want to go.

If you're sufficiently worked up and feel it's justified, sneak in there and take it. But first, take a few minutes to write down why you are taking away said article and when you intend to give it back. This exercise will help to avoid knee-jerk (emphasis on the "jerk") reactions that you will almost instantly regret. It will also make you think through exactly why you are enforcing this particular punishment, reassure your teen that the missing cell phone is in your possession and not in the wash cycle, and provide him with a way/date/time to get it back, thus preventing wholesale hysteria.

I am a writer so this comes naturally to me, but I honestly believe that if more parents routinely communicated with their teens through writing, there would be a lot more harmony on the home front. Just a tiny plug for literacy.

JUST WALK AWAY, RENEE . . .

Patience is a virtue, but it's not one of mine. This simple sanity-saver comes to you with fervent wishes that you'll be far better at applying it than I am.

When you're in a heated discussion (i.e., a full-scale meltdown) with your teen, take a deep breath, stop talking, and count to ten. This will go a long way toward defusing a rapidly disintegrating situation. Or if you're too enraged to count, just shut your mouth for a minute or two. My husband is super-accomplished at this shutting-down tactic, which makes him a very annoying mate at times, but a superb parent of adolescents. If he's sufficiently upset, he can literally not talk for days. Lulu should be so lucky with me.

In the dance of anger, it takes two to tango. If you stop cold, there is no way your teen can keep the rage-fest going. He'll have to change his steps or do a solo performance, which is not nearly as satisfying as a dual-action, full-blown argument. If you are as immature as me, you're probably asking, *"Why should all this be up to me? Why do I have to be the one to change? I'm the parent. What's wrong with expecting my kid to exert a little self-control?"*

The answer is that she can't. Or won't. And you're the adult, so you have to lead the way and model mature behavior like self-control.

The weird thing about anger is that it flares up in response to feeling powerless and out of control, yet it's almost completely ineffectual in changing that dynamic, particularly with teenagers. For one thing, teens love to piss you off, as I've mentioned before. And when you're seeing red, it's hard to think clearly and creatively in order to move toward a solution.

Looking back, I can see that the things that made me go totally ballistic weren't even very important. At the time I felt they were huge, frightening signs that my daughter was completely incorrigible and on the verge of disaster, when in fact she was only being a normal flaky teen. Perspective is the antidote for anger, but unfortunately it's the first thing to evaporate in the fury of the moment. And the more you say in anger, the more you'll be left with a crushing regret for what a lousy parent you've been and all the things you would change if only somebody would give you the chance to do it again properly.

When your teenager is pushing all your buttons, silence is the only possible route to peace. If that proves impossible, remember the old boxing command when combatants are told: "Go to your separate corners." Whichever parent is less likely to combust gets to be the referee and separate the pugilists. My husband routinely intervenes whenever Lulu and I are escalating well past the "healthy exchange of ideas" floor and heading for the "through the roof" penthouse. Particularly for girls and their mothers, this advice is worth its weight in gold.

Finally, if you do totally lose control of yourself with your teen, apologize. Your teen needs to see that you are willing to admit when you've made a mistake, take responsibility for your actions, and make amends. Saying "I'm sorry" is the only thing I'm really good at, perhaps because I've had lots of practice. It would be great if I could develop a consistent, or even occasional, ability to stand down. And model the power of restraint.

Agonizing Example

When Carla's stepson Zachary was about 16, he got furious at his dad about something simple—like a request that he clear his dinner plate. After a tense showdown, Zach stalked away muttering bitterly, "When I have kids, I'm never going to be a father like you. I'd rather die."

Carla's husband simply ignored the remark, but Carla was new to the adolescent game and brainlessly waded right into the fray.

"How dare you say that! Do you have any idea of everything your dad does for you?"

Naturally, Zach's response to her was "Fuck off."

And her husband's response was "Just stay out of this, Carla. I don't need you defending me."

Carla burst into tears and retreated to the kitchen to wash the pots and pans as loudly and furiously as possible.

Ten years later, Carla's own daughter Annabelle became a teen, and with a decade of teen trauma under her belt, Carla realized that her husband had the correct approach after all. When Annabelle haughtily informed her mother the other day that she was going to be a parent as unlike her as possible, Carla simply laughed and said, "Time will tell, honey bun."

ARE THEY
DOING THIS ON PURPOSE?

One of my all-time favorite movie scenes occurs near the end of *The Witches of Eastwick*. Rascally Jack Nicholson, having had his way with three beautiful women and impregnated each with his demon seed, is struck down by their witchy powers. Crawling into a Sunday church service, wracked by their evil spells, he screams at the dazed parishioners, "What I want to know is when God made women, did he make a mistake? Or did he do it on purpose?!"

That pretty much encapsulates my existential question about teenagers. Are they acting this way because it's pure instinct to be as loathsome as possible? Or are they trying to drive you crazy on PURPOSE?

I've decided the answer is . . . yes.

Teenagers act on pure impulse about 90 percent of the time; they're simply flailing about trying to figure out who they are. Their brains are enmeshed in a panic over splotchy skin eruptions, if they're ever going to get laid, whether they're going to miss the Party of the Year because of your ludicrous rule about parents having to be home, and why they have to go to college since they already know everything important there is to learn.

And yet, they also quite purposefully decide that you are the bane of their existence and what they must fight like hell against becoming. Teens are compelled to figure out who they are in direct opposition to you. For a parent, this process is both draining and maddening. You are being rejected to a degree that brings to mind the worst days of middle school— in fact, the whole experience may well make you relive your own tortured adolescence. (My sister, the shrink, told me that the age at which teens pose the most trouble for their parents is likely to be the same time period that was most difficult for the parents during their *own* adolescence. How exquisite a torture!)

Don't deny your feelings of anger at this predicament, but try to access the deeper emotions of loss and fear that are part of letting your child go. Chances are, you're a fair distance from Acceptance (you get to go through Depression and Bargaining first), but just knowing that anger is a natural part of the grieving process should help to alleviate a bit of your helpless confusion.

Some days, raising an adolescent is like being hit by a truck that backs up and drives over you, again and again. On *purpose*. I quite agree.

Stage 3: Depression

AGES 12–18,
THE HELLACIOUS PERIOD

WHILE ANGER IS THE MOST OBVIOUS EMOTIONAL response to adolescence, depression is probably the most pervasive and long-lasting. Its onset is a logical reaction to loss—that is, to your beloved child growing up and doing everything he or she can to get as far away from you as possible. Those days when she used to wrap her arms around your neck in affection are gone forever, replaced with her desire to rap herself into a hip-hop coma. His once-sunny, freckled face is barely recognizable now in the sullen mask that reveals nothing more than the wish that you'd stick your well-meaning advice "where the sun don't shine."

Depression is also inherent in the disappointment you're bound to feel at the end of the elementary school rainbow. That dazzling spectrum promised that every child—*your* child!—was extraordinary and destined for great things, and you believed it. Yet halfway through the dull migraine known as middle school, you realize the far more likely scenario is that your progeny will be only average (like you). This prospect of utter normalcy hits you like a sledgehammer, pulverizing your fancy dreams. Your son is probably not headed for the Major Leagues since he weighs about ninety-five pounds and has refused to practice any fielding skills since last year. And apparently, your daughter is not destined for the Ivy League unless they start requiring AP scores in Facebook. It would be bad enough if your teens were headed toward lives of quiet desperation, but somehow they feel the need to constantly demonstrate the depth of their angst. Yes, these are the times that try parents' souls.

The depression seeping into your soul is further inflamed by the realization that when your child becomes an adult it means, de facto, that you are old and ready to die. Your biological imperative for existence on the planet has been accomplished; it's pretty much a quick jump from here to managed care. Sob!

At this point, it's important to acknowledge one universal truth: Living with teenagers is depressing. Their attitude is depressing. Their rooms are depressing. Their irresponsibility is depressing. Their lack of gratitude is depressing. Their contempt is depressing. Their near-constant need for conflict is depressing.

One of the most insidious aspects of depression is thinking that every other parent's life is super-upbeat, positive, and rewarding while yours resembles the Death March of Bataan. This segment of the book will cheerfully counter that mistaken belief. It will examine some of the many, many causes of parental depression, reassure you that almost every parent feels equally unequal to the task of living with a snotty teenager, and give you some strategies to cope with feeling overwhelmed, unappreciated, and under-medicated.

7

"Worst-Case Scenario" Is Sugarcoating It

Agonizing Example

Robert and Betsy met and married in college and have been madly in love their whole adult lives. Robert is a film producer and Betsy is the human relations director of a large corporation. Of their two boys, one graduated and went off to college, only to drop out and move home during his junior year. He basically hasn't left the basement for the past three years. The other son became a skinhead at age 14, got arrested four times, dropped out of high school, and is only now aspiring to a job at Subway, for which his parents are insanely grateful. The youngest daughter is a gifted fencer and a great student, now in college getting straight A's. Robert and Betsy hope her success lasts, the Subway job sticks, and they get their basement back sometime in the next decade.

In my own blended family, we have one charming son who is on the ten-to-twenty-year plan to finish his teaching degree, one daughter who is a brilliant scholar and entirely self-motivated, and one son who is somewhere in the wilds of Idaho, where hopefully the presence of barnyard animals will inspire him to finish high school. And then there's my darling Lulu, about whom I can write anything since she loathes reading and will never voluntarily pick up this or any book.

So much for the myth of genetics. Apparently it's not nature or nurture. It's Vegas, baby—and anything can happen.

This wasn't the outcome we expected when we read our adorable toddlers mentally stimulating books every night, jump-started kindergarten through fourth grade, and saved assiduously for the college tuitions they may never use. But there are no guarantees when it comes to your children. Some kids sail through adolescence with very few problems, and some hit it like a Mack truck going sixty miles per hour into a sand trap. If your little one is stubborn, oppositional, and defiant, the teen years are likely to be a challenge. If your child loves to please, is self-directed, and goes with the flow, you may get off easy. Yet rare is the family that cruises through adolescence without a hitch. And if you have more than one child, your odds of escaping adolescent agony are almost nil.

WHEN BAD KIDS
HAPPEN TO GOOD PEOPLE

If you're the parent of an academically gifted, soccer-playing, cancer-curing teen, chances are you'll flip right over this section. Your kid couldn't remotely be considered bad and obviously, bad kids happen only to lousy parents—the kind of parents who never go to church, toss their beer cans into the front yard, and wear slippers all day.

I'm sure some of that is true; many kids who run off the rails do come from families with a lot of difficulties and dysfunction. And a lot of kids who go postal come from families that are 100 percent nuclear, close-knit, pie-eating folk. Not to mention that there's still plenty of time for your perfect cherub to develop a severe eating disorder, have a nervous breakdown, or go goth on your ass. So don't tempt fate by thinking you're immune. Nobody's immune.

The real question is: Is it your fault if your teen is a disaster?

Answer: Probably no more so than when your teen turns out brilliantly.

My theory is that teenagers are primarily manifesting their own destinies, derived from who they are and what issues they need to resolve on this revolution of the wheel of life. Of course, this Betty-as-Buddha philosophy is easy to swallow when your child is doing well; it's incredibly difficult to choke down when he's going to hell in a hand-basket. There is literally nothing more depressing than watching your child refuse to live up to his potential, squander his talents in defiant behavior, or make choices that may narrow his choices in the future.

And then there's that terror you feel that perhaps your child's destiny *is* to become a multiply-pierced cashier with a passion for daytime TV. Will you then have to learn to enjoy endless reruns of *Hollywood Squares* so you'll have something to talk about? Can that, God forbid, be *your* parental destiny?

Don't throw in the towel quite yet. It's not over until it's over and teenagers are shape-shifters to an astonishing degree. Plenty of horrendous adolescents do manage to pull up and fly right, creating great lives for themselves and becoming contributing citizens of society. It could happen—and then you can take total credit for that.

WORDS OF WISDOM

In my friend Frank's experience, children come into this world with their personalities fully intact. When his oldest daughter Eliza was born, they handed her right to Frank because his wife was drugged out of her mind from the delivery. As he was holding his new daughter in his arms, Eliza opened her eyes, took one look around, mewed a little, then went straight back to sleep. And she's been like that ever since—she's the most easy-going, well-adjusted person Frank knows. When his second daughter Jasmine was born, the nurses handed her to Frank, she opened her mouth and started to scream. And she has been hollering and demanding attention ever since. Frank's two daughters are as different as night and day, and it never ceases to amaze him that the same two people produced two such utterly opposite children.

IT'S THE EXPECTATIONS, STUPID

Dashed expectations = depression. Unfortunately, parental expectations come in all shapes and sizes, so there are oodles of them to be dashed. Expectations of what your family life will be like. Expectations that this journey is supposed to be easy and enjoyable. And expectations you have of your kid . . . the big land mine.

Some experts tell us that children will rise to the level of our expectations—as if all kids were equally buoyant—while talk-show hosts advise that requiring too much of children will cause them to hate you forever. Logically I understand that when you lower your expectations, you increase your

happiness by about 1,000 percent, making you a more relaxed and loving parent. Yet for some of us overexpecters,
lowering the bar ranks right up there in the pantheon of parenting sins with serving trans fats and not attending back-to-
school night.

Clearly, expectations are tricky and slippery as mercury.
Should they be high? Low? Somewhere in between?

I think the answer is to start high and gradually collapse to
low, as necessary.

From the time your children are toddlers, until middle
school, it is important that you articulate that you believe
they are capable of achievement. They need to know you believe in them, that getting a good education is a core value of
your family, and that doing their best is Job #1—all messages
they will ferociously reject and hopefully internalize. Some
kids will take the ball from there and run with it. Other kids
will lie down on the field and let themselves be trampled. Depending on which type of kid you have, you may have to
gradually adjust your expectations before they are crushed
out of you.

If your teen is a driven overachiever, you'll have to figure
out how much latitude to give her so she doesn't stress herself
silly with competitive fervor. If your kid is a classic under-
achiever, it is pointless and heartbreaking to keep expecting
him to transform into an honor-roll student or star athlete. By
all means, encourage him to do his best and create a structure
that promotes that. Just don't let yourself get caught up in believing that every kid is meant to excel. That, my friend, is the
road to disappointment.

Being disappointed in your teenager is bad. It's wrong. And
it's almost inevitable, since teenagers don't give you much to
admire about their "character." They're also unlikely to be
exhibiting many of the habits of highly successful people. Yet

when you're disappointed in your child, what's hard at work is primarily *your* ego. It's no secret that your children are a reflection of you—the ultimate expression of both your parenting skills and your genetic contribution. But holding your children responsible for making you look good is not highly evolved parenting. In your heart you know that your teens' ultimate task is to become the best, most true expression of *themselves.*

If you're like some folks, it's a daily struggle to move beyond the glorious dream of your child's future that you want and feel entitled to maintain. The question you need to ask yourself is whether this fantasy is depriving you of the genuine experience of your kid's unique qualities. You can look at other people's kids and think, *"Why? Why do they get the athlete and I get the quitter? Why is their kid brilliant and motivated and mine is lackadaisical and indifferent? Why do they get the debate captain and I get the detention champion? WHY?"* Or you can do some serious mind control and think, *"I wonder what my kid's unique talents are." "It's going to be fascinating to see where her amazing social skills lead her." "Wow, he's really learning to deal with adversity this year."*

I know it's hard. And it's depressing to have to give up the ideal of a perfect kid who is going to make you look awesome. But give it up you must, or suffer the ultimate disappointment—which would be engendering his life-long resentment for your inability to accept him for who he is, or realizing that you are responsible for her crushing lack of self-confidence. Focusing on what your teen *can* control (effort and attitude) is hugely preferable to harping on what he may find completely overwhelming (accomplishments and results). It's also more realistic and compassionate to concentrate on the process, not the finish line.

WORDS OF WISDOM

I love to garden. Back in my old house, I had four or five beautiful flower beds I worked on slavishly, plus a big vegetable garden. One early morning I was walking through the dew-dipped backyard, enjoying the dawn. I started to worry about the moonflowers that hadn't yet bloomed. I noticed the wild rose was falling off the trellis. Some fungus seemed to be attacking my cherry tomatoes. And the dahlias weren't as big as they should be, either.

Suddenly I thought: What the hell is wrong with me? My garden was filled with blooming flowers, budding vines, and plump vegetables, but instead of delighting in that, I could see only problems. Looking for the bad and overlooking the far greater good. And immediately I thought, that's exactly the kind of parent I am, too. Every day I should remind myself: I have an amazing, beautiful daughter with a great spirit, a kind heart, and a glorious joyfulness. Plus three stepchildren who are amazing people. Bemoaning anything that these children are not manifesting is just pure lack of gratitude.

The cosmic shift between delighting in your child and judging your child is a natural result of realizing that your ability to shape him is coming to an end. Whenever you're feeling depressed about how your kid is doing, instead of looking at what he's not accomplishing, compare him to all the kids in detention, rehab, and juvenile hall. Look downward, angel.

WHY CAN'T WE
ALL JUST GET ALONG?

I grew up in a very close family of eight kids. We had dinners together, said family prayers every night, did our homework together on the kitchen table, and played giant games of croquet, football, and badminton in the backyard. Amidst all this congeniality, one night when my parents were away, my older brother threw my oldest sister down a full flight of stairs because she wouldn't give him back his toothbrush. (She survived unscathed; her monster curlers probably broke her fall.) Another night, my father became so enraged at my sister (who was pretty much hysterical from ages 12 through 18) that he chased her, screaming in terror, around the dinner table with a broom while the rest of us looked on in fascinated horror and my mother pleaded for amnesty.

The myth of the perfect family is just that: a myth. And how depressing is that?

People who live together experience conflict, no matter how it's expressed. Some families are volatile and verbal; others are quiet and seemingly unflappable. Whatever your family's emotional style, during the teen years things are likely to get a lot worse—to the point where abandoning the homestead begins to feel like a heroic lifesaving measure. You loathe your kids, you can't stand your mate, the kids are vicious monsters to one another, and there is not one person in the family with whom you are speaking.

As issues with your child become increasingly more complex, you and your mate are unlikely to agree on every parenting decision. Easy consensus questions like "Shall we take Kiddie Yoga?" will morph into incendiary ones like "How the hell did he manage to flunk phys ed? Did he get that lack of coordination from *you*?" Tensions flare. In this maelstrom,

AGONIZING EXAMPLE

Teen wants to bring the current love interest on a family ski weekend.

Hard-Ass tells Teen he can't because it's a family weekend and the love interest is not in the family (and hopefully not in the family way, either).

Teen goes directly to The Enabler, becomes teary-eyed and wounded over the insensitivity of Hard-Ass, and professes a lack of interest in continuing to live.

The Enabler then stomps in and pressures Hard-Ass to change the decision that was made unilaterally and is therefore not binding.

Hard-Ass refuses to budge and threatens to call off the weekend entirely.

Pre-Teen overhears this threat to the weekend and screams that Teen and Hard-Ass always ruin everything.

The Enabler agrees with Pre-Teen and reiterates the demand that Hard-Ass change the decision and salvage the weekend plans.

Hard-Ass, feeling cornered, frostily informs Teen and The Enabler that nothing is going to be changed in this goddamn household except underwear.

And . . . we're off to the races.

one parent will traditionally take on the role of Hard-Ass and the other The Enabler. This division can lead to some powerful negative undercurrents that remain years after the rapids of adolescence are behind you.

Hard-Ass generally resents the crap out of The Enabler, who will not hold the line and constantly caves in to the teenager, thus making Hard-Ass look like the bad guy, instead of the only person in the goddamn family who's being consistent and firm and upholding the rules and structure. The Enabler can't believe what a hard-ass the Hard-Ass is being, when it's obvious that a little bit of love and compassion would go a long way toward making the kid feel good about himself, and why blow up every single issue into a huge battle? Often, these roles are gender-specific, with Dad being the Hard-Ass and Mom acting as The Enabler, but there are plenty of households (including mine) where it's an equal-opportunity transgender experience.

Of course, teenagers are master manipulators and quickly learn to play their parents like a harpsichord.

The only way to avoid this splintering effect is for both parents to present a united front and not give in to the nearly irresistible desire to verbally bash each other. Of course, presenting a united front means that you are either in harmony with your mate about how to deal with your obnoxious teen, heavily medicated, or willing to compromise your opinions for the sake of peace. (And if compromise was easy, we'd have tranquillity in the Middle East and freedom in Tibet, so don't feel too badly if you discover that you'd rather fight than give in.)

Despite the illicit thrill of being able to instigate it, teens will experience their parents disparaging one another as a disturbing conflict of loyalties (because way down deep, they love and feel themselves to be part of both of you). It will also allow them to pit you against each other like nobody's business. So get used to whispering savagely at each other behind closed doors, then come out smiling. Hypocrisy is no crime, and pretending to like each other should be practiced rigorously by all members of the household.

Especially siblings, since no one on earth can hurt you more than your brothers and sisters. I have seven; I should know. From the day the first-born has to stand aside and watch his parents coo adoringly over the insufferable second child, the seeds of conflict and undying connection are sown. Siblings have years of experience in making you laugh or pissing you off, and you're hardwired to react to the things they say and do. When they decide to go for the jugular, they rarely miss.

Watching your kids snipe at one another can be even more depressing than finding yourself in the line of fire. Sibling conflicts can swiftly escalate into full-scale hysteria (girls) or brutal physicality (boys), tipping the household into utter pandemonium. As tempting as it can be to wade into the fray, it's essential that you resist the urge. Once you enter the ring, the conflict will become a total free-for-all and your family will disintegrate into something resembling the Balkan States. Instead, separate the combatants and demand that they shut it down. That's about the most refereeing you should do.

If you're disciplining one child and the other kids decide to weigh in with their opinions of your parenting skills, separate yourself and the disciplinee from the peanut gallery and continue your process. There is absolutely no winning when you're trying to hold the line with one teen while fending off critiques from two or three others.

As discouraging as it can be to witness your children turn into cannibals with each other during the teen years, remember that this, too, is a stage. They won't fight bitterly forever, and often the ones who fight the most end up being closest. Observe what happens when anyone outside the family gets into conflict with one of your kids. Do the siblings band together and form a united front? Rush in to defend each other? Ferociously coalesce? Try to comfort yourself with the knowledge that if your kids didn't love each other so much, they wouldn't feel free to lash out and attack each other, comfortable in the

TALES FROM POST-TEENS ● ● ● ● ● ● ●

My parents didn't say too many dumb things to me; I guess I'm lucky. My parents were idiots, though, when they thought we couldn't hear or understand when they fought with each other. They were probably too open about what they didn't like about each other and didn't always give us positive ideas about the other one. (They got divorced when my little sister left for college.) I even knew enough to tell them not to fight around us. That was really thoughtless of them, and my relationship skills are probably forever ruined. Oh well, I guess we came out okay.

knowledge that there is no way they could possibly lose that relationship.

Finally, deal only with today's unpleasantness. Looking down the road to your funeral service and the horrific fight your children will probably have *at your graveside* is rather pointless. Don't add fuel to the fire of their arguments and when necessary, leave the house. They probably won't kill each other and at the very least, you'll be spared their fury. Sometimes that's the most you can hope for.

TODAY IS THE FIRST DAY
OF THE REST OF YOUR DEPRESSION

If you're as old and haggard as me, you probably remember the infamous *Desiderata* poem that was enormously popular in the early '70s and hung on the back of a million dorm-room doors: "Go placidly amid the noise and the haste. . . ." That poster depressed me so badly, I can't tell you. No matter how stoned I was, I didn't believe a word of it, much less think I was capable of manifesting any of the requested behavior.

Sometimes I feel the same way about people urging parents to be upbeat and positive during these appalling teen years. Let's face it: All the best days of parenting are behind you. What's left is slogging through a swamp of rejection and worry with nothing to look forward to except another crappy report card and a Hummer-full of attitude about how you're ruining their life.

Agonizing Example

I was sitting in an airport the other day and saw a young boy squealing with delight as he watched a plane pull up to the gate. He was so excited, he began whacking his father's knee and exclaiming, "Daddy, Daddy, look! The plane is coming in! That's our plane! It's so big! And it's red! And we get to go on it!!!" The mom smiled wearily at me over her toddler's bouncing head but the dad was oblivious, trying to sit there and read his *USA Today* in peace. I wanted to grab his arm and yell, "Listen up, dude. You're going to blink and that boy's joy will have evaporated and he'll be just another thug in a hoodie with his iPod on, and you will never, ever be able to recapture this time when he's filled with joy and happiness and adores you. So if I were you, I would put down that paper and treasure this moment!" Of course, he'd probably have called the Transportation Security Administration to have me arrested as a terrorist so I just sat there drinking my coffee, enjoying the boy's wild enthusiasm and feeling extremely blue.

Joyful toddler scenarios like this are so far from what you're experiencing with your teenager, it almost brings tears to your eyes. Your teen wouldn't be able to conjure up that much enthusiasm if you were presenting her with her own Lear jet; she'd probably just be pissed off that the interior was the wrong color. You think of all the happy, fun times you spent making Halloween costumes and Easter eggs, tickling her until she shrieked with laughter, or singing him to sleep. Those were the days. And they're gone.

Boo hoo. What's a parent to do? Drowning your sorrows leaps to mind but unfortunately, alcohol is a depressant. Praying is good. Watching old family movies is painful but satisfying. I admit, this is not the optimistic "sunny side" I previously urged you to stay on. But some days, it's important just to acknowledge how badly your life sucks and wallow in your depression before you can shake yourself off and get sunny again.

It is sadly true that this stage with your teen is bound to be monumentally depressing. And it's going to stay that way for a while, but not forever. Just when you think it can't get any worse, inexplicably your teen will throw his arm around your shoulders and say, "Love you, Dad" or "Thanks for everything, Mommy!" That'll cause the dark clouds to lift for a moment and keep you going for another endless year or so.

8

WHY BOTHER?

TEENAGERS GO SO FAR OUT OF THEIR WAY TO IGNORE you that you may begin to suspect you do not exist. In my opinion, this situation is a tragically overlooked symptom of depression. I believe the query "Are you sure you exist?" should be added to the list of warning signs alongside "Have your sleep patterns changed?" and "Did you gain or lose weight in the last three months?"

Once you realize you're experiencing feelings of nonexistence, a normal response might be to turn to your mate for validation of your physical reality. However, the teen years are often so difficult on the marital bond, it is entirely possible that your mate is also giving you the "silent treatment." And so, your feelings of not existing within the four walls of your previously nurturing and cozy domicile are painfully compounded. While some people respond to this negating behavior by lashing out, many folks become morose and immobile, with a penchant for watching too much *Oprah*.

In fact, I think it was on *Oprah* that I saw an historical overview of Reverend Jesse Jackson's career, including one of his wonderful pep talks to inner-city children. It culminated in Jesse exhorting thousands of kids to pump their little fists in the air and exclaim together, "I AM somebody!" The swell of young voices and the power of the words were incredibly emotional and rousing, and filled me with longing.

Of course, I fully realize that my puny, white, middle-class parenting problems don't amount to a hill of beans in this crazy world where many people have far more formidable issues to face everyday, but that doesn't mean I wasn't moved to tears by this heartfelt declaration. In fact, I was so inspired, I leaped to my feet, upsetting my bowl of buttered popcorn (and yes, I have gained some weight in the past three months) and chanted, "I AM somebody! I AM somebody!"

"You are somebody *lame*," one of my teenagers snidely remarked from the other room.

Once I recovered from that slight, I found it weirdly comforting to realize that my existence is of almost no consequence to my teenagers. They don't despise me all the time—because they never think of me *at all*, except when I am actively ruining their life with requests to clean up their room. When people ask me if my kids mind that I'm writing a book largely based on my experiences with them, I have to laugh. Their level of interest in anything I do is zippo. I've gone from being the very center of their existence—the life-giving mother—to an occasional embarrassment behind the wheel of a vehicle taking them where they want to go.

Teenagers' most telling characteristic is total self-absorption. It's annoying as hell to live with, but there is freedom in that posture, as well as a model for you to practice. Put yourself first and try to forget they exist for an hour or two a day. It's easier than you think.

You *are* somebody!

CAUTION:
ZERO-GRATITUDE ZONE

It's a simple and sadistic equation: The more parents do for teenagers, the less teens appreciate it. And of course, the less likely they are to do anything they are asked. Much as I'd like to blame them, it's our fault. We've raised them to behave this way.

For instance, the times I've become most enraged with Lulu (followed immediately by plummeting, guilt-fueled depression) are the times I've done far more for her than I should have, and she responds with callous indifference, a demand for even more indulgence, or a seriously snotty attitude. I call it the "Super Sweet 16" Syndrome, based on the hideous MTV show in which some horrid child is thrown a $100,000-plus birthday party and proceeds, inevitably, to act like the spoiled rotten brat he or she is.

Once you've started down the Path of Overdoing It, you can't get off without a cosmic shift in your household dynamic that will be received with all the openness of the Whitewater Commission. Overindulgence requires more and more incremental work to keep the status quo rolling. And when you've rendered your child helpless by doing everything for him, it does not bode well for any kind of sustainable future in which cooking, cleaning, or actual work is required. If you think I'm exaggerating, note that recent studies reveal this crop of teenagers lags in maturity almost four years behind the previous generation (making Gen-Xers look like super-motivated coffee achievers).

Most teens are emotionally and domestically retarded and that's infuriating, for sure. They don't appreciate your wonderful house. They don't appreciate your multiple cars. They don't appreciate the buffet of high-definition TVs, iPods, cell phones, video games, and computers at their fingertips. They don't appreciate the good food you serve and the great vacations you plan. They don't appreciate the education you've killed yourself to earn for them. They don't appreciate their closets full of clothes or the jobs you'll help them get. Particularly if *you* were raised in a household where almost none of this was provided, you're likely to feel horribly jealous of your own children for what they have and you didn't—and doubly furious at their sense of entitlement.

Yet why should they feel indebted to you? Teens are opportunistic to the bone and know that you would gladly hurl yourself in front of a truck to protect their sorry butts. The idea of gratitude is as foreign as quails' eggs to them. They consider your servitude their birthright, and whatever they can get away with is fair game. If you're honest, you'll have to admit that you treated your parents the same way. The difference is, our parents were smart and cheap enough not to indulge us in much beyond the basics of room, board, and a few clothes.

If the zero-gratitude dynamic truly bothers you, stop buying your kid so much crap and make them do a few chores. Or wait and watch the world teach your grown child a lesson or two about the way things work. Sure, it will probably take your kids a good decade to realize how much they owe you; waiting for gratitude is the ultimate exercise in delayed gratification. But by then, you'll be so thrilled to have them out of the house and the electroshock treatments will have been so successful, you'll hardly remember this age of agony.

TALES FROM POST-TEENS • • • • • • • • •

My parents were sort of hippies, so they raised us in a counterculture atmosphere. We had a big, rambling house out in the country and my mother used to grow all-organic vegetables that we'd eat on plates that my dad made on his pottery wheel. They didn't believe in giving us a lot of material things, which was okay but they also didn't believe in modern media. So we had the smallest TV ever made—it had like a 9" screen. They didn't want us to enjoy TV and on that set, we didn't. You were better off reading or going outside to play. Looking back, I can see it was a brilliant strategy but at the time we thought we were so deprived we should be in foster care. Now I've got a new baby, and my wife and I are fighting about whether he should be watching any TV—I'm totally opposed to it and can't stand the idea that he's going to grow up feeling entitled to high definition and addicted to cable. Apparently, I have become my parents—how bizarre is that!

THE UNKNOWABLE TEEN MIND

It's a beautiful Saturday afternoon. Your daughter went to a party last night, slept in, has a minimal amount of homework, and is planning to go out tonight. You think you're all having a pretty nice day. Yet when you walk in her room to ask her what time she wants a ride to the movies, she unloads on you like a ton of bricks. "Can't you see that I'm doing something right now?" (That would be slathering gel in her hair.) "Just leave me alone!"

Huhhh?

What bug is biting her butt?

You can feel the veins in your forehead begin to throb because seriously, what does she have to be upset about? Her life is a total cakewalk and by the way, why isn't she doing any of her chores? You haven't asked a single thing of her all day, and this is how she repays you? Her room is a pigsty but she's obviously aching for a fight and you don't have the energy to go chastise her about it. You've got a good mind to walk back in there and ground her.

Then you start to worry.

Maybe something is seriously wrong.

Maybe her phantom boyfriend is mad at her.

Maybe she got left out of something at school and she's feeling terribly insecure.

Maybe she's flunking school and doesn't know how to tell you.

Maybe she's getting expelled and figures the best defense is a good offense.

Maybe she went "all the way" with the phantom and now he's avoiding her.

Maybe the idea of taking the SATs is scaring her to death.

Maybe she's having an anxiety attack about applying to college.

Maybe she's seriously depressed and is in there contemplating SUICIDE!

Mothers are the only ones who run this kind of tragedy triathlon, of course. Dads are likely to blithely conclude, while flipping through a couple of football games and a soccer match, "Honey, she's in a rotten mood. Leave her alone until she gets over it." (Obviously, he's inured to the pain of living with a moody female.)

Now that you're worried about the dark portents of your teen's mood, you wonder how you can get her to confide in you and tell you what's wrong. You know if you were a good mom, she'd be talking your ear off about all her deepest feelings. That's how it goes down in the movies when Hilary Duff is having a meltdown and her mom walks in. The two of them end up sitting on the bed having a good heart-to-heart and hugging each other before they head downstairs for some hot cocoa. Why can't your life be like that?

Ignoring your husband, who is deep in a sports coma and hasn't registered that you're doing exactly what he just counseled you against, you head back into her bedroom and say gently, "Honey, what's wrong? I just want to know that you're okay."

"Mom! What's wrong is that you won't get out of my face! Now leave me *alone*!"

Why can't teens tell you what's wrong with them?

Well, one answer is that they don't know. Their feelings are so huge and tumultuous, they slosh over the kids like a tidal wave. Teens literally don't realize what hit them; they're just angry and resentful and want to lash out at someone. And that someone is you. Not knowing why they're feeling what they're feeling is a special provenance of boys, as anyone who's picked up a psychology magazine in the last ten years is keenly aware. Boys are prone to suffer from a low Emotional Quotient (EQ), which means they're hopelessly estranged from every single one of their feelings. You'd be better off asking your basset hound to explain what's going on in that big, sad head of his.

Another possibility is that teens won't tell you what's bothering them simply because you want to know. Withholding information from their parents is one of the few arenas over which teens have complete power. When they're feeling at the end of a crack-the-whip chain of burdensome responsibilities, one more parental request for divulgence of personal information is likely to break the camel's back.

So, if you pretend that you *don't* want to know what they're thinking and feeling, will teens suddenly begin to confide their innermost secrets?

No, sorry, it doesn't work that way. They may feel slightly less inclined to barricade themselves against your intrusion, but many teens can literally go for *years* without sharing any personal information with their parents. (I know I did, but my parents didn't seem to notice or mind one bit.) Content yourself with the knowledge that there's not much of interest going on in their heads anyway.

And stop watching Hilary Duff movies.

Parents Are from Venus; Teens Are from That New Planet Beyond Pluto

Between the ages of 15 and 16, your teenage son or daughter is likely to do something so excruciatingly moronic and self-destructive, it will literally take your breath away. Possibilities include but are not limited to: stealing a car (before getting a license), breaking and entering (probably one of your friends' homes), flunking a class or getting suspended/expelled from

Agonizing Example

My friend Diane's son had a devastating car accident in which his Jeep Wrangler was hit broadside at about fifty miles per hour and flipped into a drainage ditch, pinning Justin underwater, unconscious, for about five minutes. Miraculously, he escaped with a broken collarbone, punctured lung, and minor cuts and bruises. Diane was shaken to the core by her son's close encounter with death. But the day Justin was released from the hospital, she wanted to kill him herself when she saw him out in the backyard, smoking a cigarette. With a punctured lung.

school, falling in love with someone completely inappropriate, having unprotected sex, getting a tattoo on some highly visible body part, doing drugs, setting something on fire, or all of the above.

Faced with this debacle of delinquency, you will be plunged into a panic of such magnitude and duration you will question every parenting decision you've made, blame the other provider of genetic material, and/or enter long-term, bank-breaking therapy. Your child, on the other hand, will immediately forget much of this stuff happened unless you rudely remind him by punishing him, or the natural consequences continue to haunt her (upcoming trials, probation, house arrest bracelets, and so forth). Is this convenient lapse of memory a sign that your kid is incorrigible and remorseless, or is it simply the way teenagers are?

It's the troubling and mysterious way teenagers are, but much of that bizarre insensitivity is based on physiology (and

TALES FROM POST-TEENS ● ● ● ● ● ● ● ● ●

I was a pretty good kid. I didn't drink, smoke, do drugs, or miss curfew. I did my homework without being asked and other than choosing to talk back to everything my mother said, I think I was probably an easy teen. But for some reason I really wanted to drive before I was 16 so I decided to steal cars. Two, to be exact.

The first time I did it, I was with my friend Claire. We were in the drama club and at a meeting with our drama teacher about a theater festival. At one point, the teachers were all supposed to talk. Since Claire and I were the only students who had come along and it was a Saturday, we didn't have anything to do. So we told our drama teacher that we left my sweater in her car and asked for her keys. We then decided to drive her car around the parking lot. Well, to make matters worse, when I was driving I got so freaked out that I peed in my pants and wet her seat. We told my drama teacher that we spilled a coke on her seat when we were reaching for my sweater. Nice, huh?

Unfortunately, I didn't learn my lesson. Later that year, my dad was out of town and my mom was in DC with a friend and stupidly left me home alone. I invited Claire over to spend the night and we decided to rent a movie. Since I lived all of 1.5 miles from Blockbuster, we decided to take my dad's car. (In neither instance did I have a license.) My dad's car was a stick shift and since I didn't know how to drive it, we went the entire way there in first gear. We got there fine (despite numerous stall-outs at various stop signs) but on the way home, I had a mishap. As I was backing out of the parking space, I hit another car. Somehow the gods were with me and no damage was done to the other car, but my dad's headlight was broken.

That night a freak snowstorm hit. I thought I'd have a reprieve of a day or two (until my father came home) to figure something out. But my mother decided to go out and clean off his car when she got home. So Claire and I are in the front yard building a snowman and I'm starting to freak out, when my mom exclaims, "Girls, look what the storm did to your father's car!"

To this day, my father thinks the storm broke his headlight. My mother, who died five years ago, must have figured it out by now and will likely ground me when I see her in heaven.

a soft frontal lobe). Ask any pediatric surgeon: Kids recover from even the most severe traumas about ten times faster than adults. Hence their cavalier bounce-back from events that leave you laid out with worry and despair.

One of the most depressing aspects of parenting a teen is feeling as if everything that matters to you—like your kid living to adulthood, for instance—is of no consequence to your teen at all. The word "disconnect" was made for days like these. (And no, my mama didn't tell me about them—or if she did, I was a teenager myself and not listening.) It's difficult to plumb the depths, or shallows, of what your kid is feeling because, as we discussed earlier, most teens are not forthcoming about their emotions. The one thing I can tell you for sure is they aren't feeling things the same way as you.

Teenagers think of themselves as immortal. Trying to impress upon them the risks and dangers of certain behaviors might as well be communicated in Sanskrit. Apparently, teens also hear things on a different frequency; one of the few decipherable sounds is the tone of another teen's voice. Example: You give your teen hundreds of harrowing lectures about the dangers of driving without a seat belt, yet still have to remind her to buckle up every time you get in the car. Then one day your teen turns to you with eyes wide and says, "Dad, you know what Jamal told me yesterday? If you hit something at sixty miles per hour and you're not using seat restraints, you'll hit the windshield with enough force to splatter your brain into shards!" Then, she'll carefully buckle herself in. Click! You are simultaneously immensely grateful to Jamal and totally resentful of the fact that he's getting total credit for the seat belt tutorial. But that's the way it goes.

The upside of teenagers not taking anything very seriously is their ability to instantly recover and move on from major disappointments—seemingly without a backward glance. All parents have had the disorienting experience of feeling buried under the weight of their teen's emotions, only to find that his or her grief evaporated in a matter of hours whereas you end up carrying the load for days. I know it's semi-impossible because you are a sensitive adult, but try to unload as fast as your teen does. Take heart in the fact that teens can bounce back from even major crises pretty darn fast. And most will live to adulthood, despite their best efforts to off themselves.

MAKING THE GRADE(S)

Ever since seventh grade when Lulu's teachers told me I should let her "fail now, before it really counts," I have been in

AGONIZING EXAMPLE

Tom's daughter Julia came home last month with a mediocre report card that featured a preponderance of Bs and Cs. Tom was pretty disappointed because he knew she could do better. He was giving Julia a pep talk about trying harder and lifting her Cs, when she went ballistic. "Dad," she screamed, "Cs are just as good as As!!" At that point, Tom thought maybe the Cs were a gift.

a flop-sweat over her academics. Of course, she was nowhere near failing; she was getting Bs and the occasional C at a highly rigorous Main Line girls' school. But in my mind, she was on the very precipice of disaster. I had no perspective on the situation then, and I have even less now that she's in high school, when it all "counts." Every time the college counselors talk about the importance of the SATs, class standing, and the mystical Grade Point Average, a shiver of panic shoots down my spine, although my fear has almost no basis in reality. Lulu has been on the honor roll or perilously close to it for most of her school years. She's a great kid and she's got a million friends. But why concentrate on all these astonishingly good things? Why not get depressed over the lack of total academic perfection and take all the other stuff for granted?

Naturally, Lulu has responded to this lava-like flow of anxiety by downgrading her interest in school performance to a studied indifference. She stonewalls me in every inquiry about her work, refuses to let me read her papers, and would rather pull out her fabulous long eyelashes than talk to me about anything intellectual. Opening a report card was a trip to hell for me, until I realized that I had to get myself under control or I was very like to ruin my relationship with my daughter. As my husband repeated endlessly, I'm the one who needed to back off and let go. I was driving her crazy in my insistence that she adopt my sky-high academic expectations as her own. Which, to put it mildly, they aren't.

Right now, like a lot of teenage girls, Lulu is not particularly driven to excel scholastically. She's driven to get her work done and get back to her far more important social life. She's not in love with learning; she's barely even embraced it yet. Because I was raised in an insanely competitive academic family, I didn't understand how she could be so casual about her grades. Being "smart" was an integral part of my identity through college and I wondered who she'd be without that label. Of course, when I stopped obsessing I could plainly see that Lulu is plenty smart and knows exactly who she is with or without the validation of a bevy of As.

In truth, maybe I'm jealous of that. That is the brilliant hypothesis of Eve Ensler, author of *The Vagina Monologues*. She loves teenage girls for their furious independence, wild spirits, and rebellious attitude. In short, she loves everything about them that we can't stand. And she suspects that deep down, mothers resent their teenage girls because they embody everything we gave up as we got older. Our crazy impetuousness. Our loud voices that we were so in love with. Our insistence that we were special, unique, and diamond bright.

She's got a point.

Lulu's not a stressed-out maniac like me, and that drives me nuts. Whenever I start worrying about how she'll accomplish the things she wants to do in life if she isn't as neurotic and obsessive as me, I can't escape the flip side of that question. What if *I* didn't have to become this way? What if her amazing resilience, great social skills, and kind heart allow her to accomplish ten times more than I ever dreamed of? Wouldn't that be ironic?

Hey wait! Is that a college admissions essay I've stumbled upon? I better get started right away.

WORDS OF WISDOM

Instead of the depressing scenario of fighting about homework every night, set up a system and enforce it. Ask for teachers' help in making sure assignments are written down someplace where you can find them and check them with your child before work begins. Provide a structure of time every day when the child needs to be working, whether he claims to have finished all his work or not. By all means, take away distractions—the cell phone, iPod, and Internet—while homework is presumably being done. This systematic approach is a big pain in the butt to regulate and will be regarded by your teen as a POW camp, but it will help him to get organized and be responsible. Once you've set up the structure, however, you need to back off.

If you can't stop the micromanagement, take yourself out of the loop and hire a tutor. It doesn't have to be a million-dollar investment; check with the faculty or admissions department of a local college and ask for a great student in the subject required. Even at $20/hour, it's good money for the student and a fantastic role model for your child. The tutor can help your kid with study skills, writing, and projects. Plus, anything he or she says will be about a thousand times more welcomed than if it came from you.

Your Work Here Is Done

As the clock of childhood ticks down and you realize that you have less and less time left at home with your kid, it's natural to try to jam as many critical life lessons into his cranium as possible. This is an almost entirely futile gesture, since at this point he's pretty much cooked and you no longer have the ability to add any more ingredients to the casserole of his personality. For me, this ghastly realization presented an irresistible opportunity to whip myself into a froth about all the things I should have forced upon Lulu when she was young and would still do what I wanted.

ॐ

I'm sure you have your own list (unless you're in much better mental health than I am), but here are a few of the missing links in Lulu's personal development with which I assail myself in the wee hours of the morning:

1. Latin (she took only two years and then I let her **drop it**)
2. Any kind of musical instruction (she can't even **read** music!)
3. Dance (it's **only** her favorite thing to do but did I force her to take lessons? No.)
4. **Ditto** with singing
5. Art (she's super-artistic but I never made her take lessons in painting, sculpture, or ceramics because I was **too busy** working)
6. Table manners and/or etiquette classes (how did **this** slip under my radar?)
7. Girl Scouts (if **only** I'd volunteered to be the leader, maybe her troop wouldn't have split up!)

8. Teen church group (I let her go to Mass with me instead—what a **sin**!)
9. Financial education (with no clue about checking, savings, credit cards, or investment, she'll probably go **bankrupt**!)
10. Cooking (how the hell is she going to **feed** herself?)

What's missing from this barrage of blame is the reality that Lulu absolutely refused to do most of the above, even when she was young and impressionable. But why did I let her get away with that? Now she no longer wants to get anything more from me than the keys to the car. She's not going to permit me to enlighten her about posture, astronomy, gardening, college applications, STDs, 401Ks, ironing, tipping, or folding a fitted sheet. My only recourse if I desperately want her to gain this knowledge is to draft my friends to tutor her, try to force her to take classes (as if), or optimistically assume that somewhere along the road to adulthood she's going to pick up what she needs to know and put it to use. Despite my ticking-time-bomb approach to parenting, there probably is time for her to learn most of what she needs to survive and God knows, she'll be a lot more open to it when it comes from another source.

Recently, I was bemoaning my omission in teaching Lulu good table manners and the Pyrrhic victory involved in turning every meal into a Miss Manners diatribe. My friend Mimi sagely replied, "You can't teach her anything at this point, Betty. But the first time her boyfriend points out that she eats too fast, it will change everything."

True, that.

She'll get her education from anybody but me, anywhere but here. As long as she gets it, I don't care about the source. I'll be off the hook!

You Are Too Old for This

If you thought you were depressed before, this last one will probably send you right over the ledge. But hang on! I mean it in a nice, empathetic way.

If your kid is a late teen, then you are at least 40 (we hope) and that is *way* too old for the kind of exhausting daily drama that is inherent in life with a teenager. Chances are, you haven't immersed yourself in a relationship so masochistic, painful, and conflicted since you were a broke and unemployed 23-year-old. Then you needed something bizarre and chaotic to fill the empty hours of the day, but now you're juggling a hefty mortgage, an angry boss, a kitchen renovation, and a bad back. You are seriously too old for this.

Your teenager intuitively knows this, but he's not about to let you use an age deferral to dodge this war. Any effort you make to bail out of the teen psychodrama will be met with an onslaught of histrionics meant to keep you knee-deep in it. At this point, you will realize that despite all his protestations and her screeching that you are the worst parent in the universe, your teen is heavily invested in keeping the insanity going, if only because he needs some company out there on the far reaches of adolescence. Either that, or she doesn't know how to disengage. And let's face it, it's scary to be alone—scarier even than keeping her pathetic attachment to you, the dorkiest parent on the planet.

You may be too old for the battles of adolescence, but your teen is too young to face it alone. So you're both in it together. And that's not as depressing as it seems.

9

LIGHTS AT THE
END OF THE TUNNEL

FOR THE PAST DECADE, MY TWO SISTERS, THEIR HUS-
bands, and their seven kids have spent Labor Day weekend
together at Mary Lou's house on the Connecticut River—
boating, barbecuing, playing volleyball, and having a blast.
Mary Lou's four girls are now grown, but my sister Susan, the
brilliant psychiatrist, had her last child, Matt, late in life. Matt
is now a senior in high school and hell-bent on driving Susan
nuts. This Labor Day weekend, Matt inexplicably refused to
leave Boston to go to Mary Lou's with the family. Susan
declined to leave him home alone (good call, Mom) and the
weekend plans ground to a halt. For thirty-six hours, a flurry
of standoff negotiations, threats, and older-brother interven-
tions were exchanged on the Boston home front. Finally, Matt
conceded to go and the party was back on, albeit foreshortened by two days.

On the very same Labor Day weekend, my husband and I were closing on a new cottage we'd just bought on the tidal marshes south of Savannah, complete with a boat, marina, and gorgeous ocean views. Lulu categorically refused to go to "the stupid swamp house you guys decided to buy without talking to me," so Larry went on ahead without us. I argued and pleaded with Lulu for twenty-four hours until she finally agreed to drive down on Saturday and return at noon on Sunday, leaving Larry in a fog of disgust over his four-day family weekend, now foreshortened to one.

People without teenagers might say, "How ridiculous! How could you let your bratty kids ruin your lives like that?" People with teenagers are likely to roll their eyes in sympathy and shared pain.

My sister Mary Lou, who has been through it *four* times before, simply says, "In the last couple years, teenagers just need to be gone. You can't stand them and they can't stand you. But insulting as it is to your intelligence, you do have to negotiate and compromise to get them to do anything. Basically, you're both holding your breath until they can leave."

The good news is that your teen will not stay this obnoxious forever. That's what veteran parents tell me anyway. As endless as the gauntlet of contempt appears to be, it is a stage—not a life sentence. The purpose of which, I believe, is to render teens so unbearable, parents willingly and gratefully let them go. Sure, it is depressing that the last years you spend with your teen are likely to be so relentlessly unpleasant, you'll get precious little opportunity to enjoy his final days at home. But most parents report that their teens return from the first few months at college a completely different person. The child they adored is returned to them a rational, respectful and appreciative semi-adult who is capable of having a conversation,

Tales from Post Teens • • • • • • • •

I was a pretty honest teen. I told my parents things that other kids wouldn't, mostly because my parents were overly accepting about everything except schoolwork. As long as I did very well in school, they didn't much care what I did with the rest of my time. Once I went to a party at an older friend's house and the cops came, so I called my dad to pick me up. I made him drive some of my friends home because no way could they drive, and one of them puked in the car on the way home. My parents were just happy that I called and didn't even get mad at me for the puke. When I look back at how cool they were about a lot of things, I wish I'd been a little nicer to them.

making eye contact, and modulating her voice—at least for an hour or so.

Wonders never cease.

WE ARE THE CHAMPIONS

Sometimes you get so buried in negativity about your child, you can't think of a single redeeming quality about him. Or you may be so panicked about the things she's doing, you can't seem to focus on anything but her problems. At this point, it's essential that you talk to *somebody* who thinks your kid is awesome and can give you the positive reinforcement you desperately need.

This champion of your kid might be somebody who's known your kid for a long time, from way back in the day when he was still cute, full of promise, and had his original personality. Or the champion may be someone who is wise and farseeing enough to recognize that the traits temporarily rendering your kid reprehensible are exactly what will make her a creative, uniquely talented adult. Sometimes it's a teacher who sees something wonderful in your child, or a grandparent who recognizes in the little snot many of your own not-originally-appreciated qualities. Of course, your spouse may also have this vision, but you probably won't be able to accept any input from him or her because it's likely to feel like a blatant attempt to suck up to the kid, undermine your shaky parenting skills, or make you look like the bad parent. I'd advise you to look for a champion a bit farther afield.

The champion is someone who consistently messages to you that your kid is going to be okay, is basically a good kid, and possesses aptitudes that you are currently blinded to. The champion has unflagging patience for listening to you bitch about the exact same thing over and over, and never exclaims, *"Why do you say you can't believe she did this? She did the same thing last week!"* No, the champion will moan with commiseration and say, *"Oh wow. You must be so depressed! But she's so funny and has such great social skills, I know she'll make her way out of this."*

The champion will find excuses for your child where there are none, gently put things in perspective, and let you know when you're being too judgmental or harsh, in a way you can hear. This level of acceptance is impossible to fake and can come only from someone who loves your child in a pure and uncomplicated way (as opposed to your five-alarm, ego-invested, hysterically intense way). I seriously do not know where I'd be without the sisters, friends, and teachers who have talked me down from the utter despair and fearful rages that have characterized my worst days of Lulu's adolescence.

Beyond the day-to-day support and succor, they've even found ways to reassure me that she will grow up to love me despite the kind of manic, negative parent I am.

Because I know how many times champions have saved my sanity, I try to do the same for other mothers. The children I've grown up around—Forrest, Dexter, Maura, Fallon, Kyla, Darby, Glennon, and all my awesome nieces and nephews—are incredibly precious to me (as are my stepkids, of course, but I'm half-responsible for them and have the same kind of passionate angst for them as I do for Lulu). I've seen the things these beloved kids have done over the years to drive their parents crazy, but it's never been anything close enough for me to write them off. They're amazing people who will do great things and become incredible adults. It's my job to remind their parents of that, as necessary.

TALES FROM POST-TEENS • • • • • • • • •

When I was almost 15 years old, my best friend's dad realized that I had gotten myself in some trouble and he had a long talk with me. I remember the gravity of the conversation and his concern. He looked me right in the eye and said basically this: "If you lie, it brings others into the fold who don't have anything to do with the situation. You amplify the pain and make matters worse. Lying gets you nowhere. You are a good person. Do good things."

I've never forgotten that talk, and even though it was hugely embarrassing, the fact that he took the time and cared enough to talk to me like an adult really meant a lot to me.

"TELL ME ABOUT
THE RABBITS, GEORGE"

In case you aren't somebody who loved *Of Mice and Men*, this phrase comes from big, slow Lenny, who could be comforted in times of anxiety by his friend George's stories about the soft, furry bunny rabbits they were going to have on a farm of their own, one rosy day in the future.

In times of teen-induced stress, I have often been reduced to Lenny-hood and beg young people of my acquaintance to tell me, over and over again, the litany of horrid, wretched things they did as teenagers and how as mature, functioning adults they deeply regret all the grief they caused their parents. Those stories almost never cease to calm me. They give me hope in a similarly rosy future in which Lulu realizes how much she loves me and deeply appreciates all the things I've done for her—a prospect that now seems as shimmering and far off as Oz.

Recently, I spent a brutal morning fighting with Lulu over my latest atrocity of replacing our soft, bland white bread with thin, chewy protein bread. This apparently has ruined her entire life. At work, I find solace in Abby's stories about how her mother used to make hearty homemade wheat bread that she and her sisters threw directly into the trash every single day on the way to school. Now (and this is the good part) she can't believe what an ungrateful shit she was, and how wonderful her mom was to provide that wholesome food. Ahhhhh!

When Tyler brings home another D in English, I make an emergency phone call to Judith so she can tell me again how she flunked high school chemistry specifically to hack off her father, then proceeded to get such mediocre grades she barely squeaked into college. Today, as the successful vice-president of a huge state university, she'll recall how methodically she underachieved and (this is the good part) how she and her dad laugh about it now as she drives him to Atlantic City once a month so he can gamble in a game he can actually win.

Every time I'm wallowing in envy of the kids who seem to be sailing through high school in a sea of straight A's and resumés glowing with leadership and service projects, I beg Robin to tell me how, as a similarly gifted teen, she was drinking every night, sneaking out of her house at 3 A.M., and having sex at 15. Now that she's trying to have kids of her own (big crescendo), she's thinking that as a mother she'll be a lot less trusting and indulgent than her own parents were.

Hopefully, when your child is done with his current stage of opposition, he too will become the person he truly is (as opposed to the cretin he is channeling). This transition brings the promise of a future filled with soft, furry bunny rabbits. You will *not* perpetually be the millstone around the neck of your teen or the Great Resented One. You will be able to spend an entire day in his presence without wanting to throttle him. You may even live to see your child regret the lunatic things she's done, and the hateful things she's said. And then, hopefully, your kids will pass along their tales of redemption to the suffering parents of the next teen generation.

CHANNEL YOUR INNER THELMA (OR LOUISE)

Several years ago, as the mother of three teenage girls and two teenage stepsons, my friend Veronica claimed that the central mystery of our time is why more mothers don't simply drive off in the middle of the night, never to be seen again. Clearly,

TALES FROM POST-TEENS • • • • • • • •

I was "head lifeguard" at a local military base, a dream job for an 18-year-old girl. One night, I went out with one of the male lifeguards. (Yes, technically, I was his boss, and as someone who now litigates employment discrimination matters, I find this facet of the story particularly horrifying. But I digress.)

Like any wise, levelheaded 18-year-old on a date with a hot lifeguard, I got very drunk and thought it would be a great idea to go back onto the military base and go skinny-dipping. So, we did, which was big fun, especially when I decided to go off the high dive a few times. Things were going great until the military police broke up our party and took us both back to the station.

I was charged with underage consumption and given a summons to appear in federal court. The police told me they were going to call my parents, but I informed them that I was 18 and I wanted to call somebody else. Wisely, I called my best friend and asked her to come pick me up, went home, told my folks I had been out late "watching a movie," and went to bed.

I thought I was clever until my dad found the summons on my dresser the next day. Of course, I got in big, big trouble.

But at the end of the summer, the week before I left for college, the only thing my dad said to me about drinking was "It's a tough bronc to ride, kiddo." That was it. But I never forgot that and I probably never will.

mothers and everything they do (laundry, cooking, cleaning, shopping, paying the bills, organizing the household, being nice, trying to make conversation, changing the sheets, mending, ironing, matching up socks, driving everybody everywhere, making doctor and dentist appointments, writing birthday cards, teaching manners, turning off lights, etc.) are not appreciated by anyone in the household. And just as clearly, no one in the house loves each other one tiny bit, and the mother's life has been totally wasted in trying to create a happy family. So why not flee? When Veronica told me this, she wasn't being wry or funny. She was deadly serious and hugely (but temporarily) depressed.

At the time, I had only a faint inkling of what Veronica was talking about. My stepson Jaime was 16 and a "handful" but he wasn't my full responsibility or my "fault" in the genetic sense, so I was able to distance myself from the full brunt of that misery. Now I get the whole exhausting and depressing scenario. Many of my friends who are recovering mothers of teens told me not to write this book because "Who the hell wants to read about something so awful?" Their position is that you simply put your head down and stagger through those years, then never look back. My friend Sophie chimed in helpfully: "There's nothing that can make your kid's adolescence any easier, Betty. You just have to suffer through it."

But perhaps there is some kind of middle ground here. Instead of longing to disappear forever, maybe taking off for a weekend several times a year would obviate the need to become a missing mom-person. Of course, this recommendation comes with the caveat that leaving your teen means that he or she will be under the supervision of someone less fanatic and controlling than you. Your teen will probably respond maturely by throwing a huge unsupervised party at your house and/or fail to do critically important homework.

Depending on how insane that prospect makes you, it may preclude your feeling as if you can go away. Ever. You might waste the entire weekend trying unsuccessfully to reach your teen on his cell phone (by the way, Mom, ringtones were invented so kids could identify your calls and ignore them). Worse, you may come home blissfully happy only to blow your top five minutes later when you discover your bed has been slept in (you refuse to consider by whom) and a mysterious substance is coating every one of your hardwood floors.

Ironically, the moms who most desperately need to get away are the very ones who feel that the world will collapse if they're not around. (I hear you, sister.) The world will not collapse. But unpleasant things may happen and depending on how you're wired to deal with that, it may simply not be worth it. I'm in awe of moms who have children who are responsible enough to be left alone, although I'm also painfully aware that they've enabled that situation by actually leaving— a risk I'm not eager or even willing to take.

The desire to flee from the grim task of dealing with your teenager is entirely natural and positively life enhancing. Even if it's a far-fetched fantasy, like strolling the beaches of Hawaii or making out with George Clooney, if it gets you through the day and out from behind the wheel of the getaway car, it's a good thing.

One thing I know for sure: Parenting a teen will permanently resolve your need for self-destruction. You've been paying it forward for years and will no longer be in the slightest danger of entering a bad relationship or becoming attracted to someone who's horrible to you. You have so been there, suffered that. In fact, I'm 100 percent sure that if Thelma and Louise had been mothers, they would never have driven off that cliff. They would have made it to Mexico and be sipping margaritas in Playa del Carmen or taking ceramics classes in San Miguel de Allende right this minute.

Happy Thoughts: They're Totally Different Away from Home

The reason that people still love your kid when he's being a total jerk at home isn't only because they remember how darling he was when he was 3. It's that he's darling *now*—he's just that way behind your back and with people outside the family. This is a staggering realization that at first blush can feel a lot like betrayal.

Agonizing Examples

You skulk into a school conference, still reeling from a debilitating screaming match with your daughter over your "insane" insistence that she pick up wet towels before they mildew her bed. In glowing terms, her teacher informs you that the aforementioned daughter is a model of helpfulness at school and has recently volunteered to lead the Habitat for Humanity club. Habitat for Humanity? After the inhumane way she treats your habitat, she's going to unleash herself on humanity?

Or, you are collapsed on the La-Z-Boy, trying to recover from an hour-long battle to get your son to rake the leaves, followed by three hours of furious raking on your own because the jerk couldn't be roused from his fourteen-hour sleep-a-thon. The phone rings and it's your elderly neighbor calling to congratulate you for raising such a thoughtful boy, who always helps her take out her recycling and trash. Hello???

Instead of being incensed that your teens obviously haven't learned that "charity begins at home," try to be grateful for any signs of social acceptability. Fact is, it's a lot easier for them to give, be mature, and act thoughtfully outside your abode. Their primal struggle with you won't allow them to do it at home. I witnessed this phenomenon first hand at the college where my husband worked. The students we were close to often came over, helped me cook, chattered away about all the fascinating courses they were taking, and baby-sat Lulu whenever I needed. Then their parents would come into town and I'd watch the students suddenly morph back into snotty teenagers, refuse to communicate, and be sullen and ungrateful when their parents tried to take them shopping or treat them to dinner. The de-evolution was breathtaking!

Yes, it is depressing that you will apparently be the last to experience your teenager's good side. But at least he *has* a good side to keep hidden from you. She apparently *is* capable of acts of kindness and moments of selflessness. This is good. This is more than you once believed possible. This is a reason to live!

Stage 4: Bargaining

AGES 16–17,
THE SEISMIC ERA

SOMETHING AMAZING HAPPENS TO TEENAGERS BE-
tween the sophomore and junior years of high school. Their
hearing is miraculously restored. Your son begins to be able
to form coherent sentences and explain why he wants to do
things instead of muttering obscenities at you from behind
locked bathroom doors. Communication with your daughter
evolves from an earsplitting rant featuring all "you" sentences
("*You've* ruined my life," "*You're* a total asshole," "*You* make
me sick!") to convincing if equally eviscerating tantrums that
feature multiple "I" sentences. ("*I* should be allowed to . . . ,"
"*I* am furious that . . . ," "*I* can't wait to get away from you so I
can . . . "). Some may look on this development as one of
questionable value, but any shrink can tell you it represents
progress. And due to this development, you become willing

to give your children previously unheard-of privileges like managing schoolwork on their own, getting a job, and deciding what to eat all by themselves.

What's the cause of this cosmic shift? Unfortunately, it's nothing you did or will get credit for. It's their environment. At school, with their peers, and in almost every outside situation, teens begin to get bombarded with decisions they'll have to make about life after graduation. Are they going to college? Which college? Are they going into the service? Which branch? Are they going to get a job? How, where, and why? Suddenly, everything is about the future—a future without parents in it.

As scary as all this may be, your teen is beginning to feel as if she has a tiny bit of control over her life (enabled in great part by the life-changing freedom of getting a driver's license). He can glimpse the end of your domination over his life. Though that picture appears awfully blurry and faraway, the mere knowledge that it's out there waiting for him to arrive offers a blessed reprieve from a life sentence spent with you. Of course, this is not an unequivocal step forward; teens will repeatedly revert back to their breathtakingly immature ways, but for consecutive moments you may have logical, productive conversations with them about school, social activities, relationships, and their hopes and dreams. Where you once believed there was nothing but an iTunes library and an X-box schematic, there appear to be a working brain and a beating heart. Astonishing!

This respite in the ground war of adolescence paves the way for the exciting fourth stage of bargaining. But don't let your guard down yet; the real fun and games begin when teens are old enough to believe they can handle life on their own. It's critically important to remember that you are still dealing with teenagers—which means you are negotiating with individuals who will delude, manipulate, and scam you if they think it will enable them to get the things they want. This does not make them bad people; it makes them . . . politicians.

And so, deal with your teens as you would a politician. Be wary, stay vigilant, cover your butt, and make sure you're not being sold the farm. Then shake their hands with delight, listen to all the great things they tell you they're going to do, and promise to give them a boatload of financial support, as well as your vote of confidence.

Let the bargaining begin!

10

GROUND RULES
You Versus Them

THE KEY TO BECOMING A GOOD NEGOTIATOR IS TO be able to quickly and accurately assess the stakes in any particular situation. Is this issue critically important to you? To the other party? What are you willing to give up to get your way? What is the other party willing to concede? And does the very use of the word "party" make your blood run cold? (Me, too.)

The best negotiators are calm, confident, and seemingly not personally invested in outcome. They are able to keep their eyes on the prize and not let unrelated issues or personal feelings distort their vision. When directly opposed, they find creative ways to new solutions and never descend into pointless conflict. Needless to say, after years of living with a raving lunatic of a teenager, you've had every one of those traits crushed out of you. Let's begin by focusing on what is essential to bring to the bargaining table—namely, a sense of perspective.

By the time your teen gets to be about 16, you may have become so accustomed to arguing about everything, you've completely lost sight of what's important to you. This is especially true if you're the parent of a girl. The passion brought to the issue of a missing bobby pin (which you apparently *moved* when you once again invaded her bedroom to *touch her things!*) is commensurate with the hysteria over when she is going to be allowed to drive. The quarrel over whether she can persuade you to buy prepackaged chocolate chip cookie dough is tackled with the identical fervor of whether you'll allow her to go to college in Switzerland. Things have gotten smushed together in one big tornado of conflict; you're going to have to take tiny baby steps back to good mental health.

LET'S MAKE A DEAL

Try to begin every negotiation with a quick internal inventory of your feelings. What is the outcome you're hoping for? What is the worst thing that might happen if you don't prevail? Can you give in on this issue without anything truly bad happening?

This flurry of queries will slow you down from the negotiation-killing-but-oh-so-satisfying parental response, "Over my dead body!" It will also help you avoid assigning overblown importance to issues that matter not one whit, yet still have the ability to totally derail your relationship with your teen. Keep in mind that the root word in overblown is "blow," as in "blowing it," "blowing your cool," and "blowing you off"— all common outcomes of the overblown parental reaction.

WORDS OF WISDOM

Take, for instance, the fight over a lights-out time.

You know he'll be exhausted tomorrow if he doesn't get to sleep before midnight and this will probably affect his schoolwork. (PROBLEM)

And of course you want him to be well-rested. (DESIRED OUTCOME)

The worst thing that can happen is that he'll be very tired. (NATURAL CONSEQUENCE)

So, his staying up late may be something you'll continue to nag him about. (COMPROMISE)

But you won't lay down the law to challenge the behavior (BARGAINING)

because . . . it's not the end of the world. (ENLIGHTENMENT)

In actual fact, very few things are the end of civilization as we know it—except the use of prepackaged chocolate chip cookie dough. You have to draw the line somewhere.

CHOOSE YOUR BATTLES (AND BATTLEFIELDS)

The second step in learning how to negotiate productively with your teen is knowing what *not* to negotiate. In other words, determining what you can let go (gasp!) and what's worth fighting about. This is a natural extension of the "end of the world" discussion above, but more specific in application.

When Lulu was 8 and people used to say "Choose your battles," I had no idea what they were talking about. I had a clear picture that my responsibility as her parent was to control pretty much everything in her life; there was almost no battle I wasn't up for undertaking. What she wore, check. What she ate, check. What she watched and listened to, check. What time she went to bed and got up, check. School, friends, church—check! Obviously, adolescence came as a very unpleasant shock. Lulu checkmated me on almost all the above issues, and I quickly realized that I would never last through six endless teen years if I didn't winnow down the list of things I was willing to fight over.

My friend Laurie put it succinctly for me: "I was sort of lazy as a parent and I let a lot of things slide that I probably shouldn't have. I didn't nag the boys too much about their grades or friends or how they spent their time. But anything that had to do with their safety, I was totally unyielding on. And eventually they got that and wouldn't even try to challenge me. They'd uphold most of those rules, sneak around a little, and get punished when they screwed up. But at least they knew where the lines were."

Sometimes that is the most you can hope for.

In choosing your battles, you have to determine your *most* important responsibilities as a parent. This cannot be done on an *ad hoc* basis; it takes some thoughtfulness and quiet reflection (meaning a time when your teenager isn't around to piss you off). Unfortunately, my list isn't quite as streamlined as Laurie's. I'm still obsessed with Lulu's schoolwork and would probably need a lobotomy to let that go, although I suspect she worries about her grades in direct inverse proportion to how much I do. I continue to bug her about what she eats. And we routinely argue about things that are ridiculously unimportant in the big scheme of things: like her habit of putting on five outfits before she finds one she likes, leaving the rejected four in a heap on the floor of her closet.

I find the greatest impediment in choosing my battles is the stuff that I'm carrying forward from my own unattractive teen years. For instance, the belief that routine household habits are a harbinger of one's character and values. This questionable ideal was hammered into me (and my seven brothers and sisters) by my German grandmother. She firmly believed that one was either the kind of person who swept things under a rug (this is not a metaphor) or the kind who fanatically lifted and swept underneath *every single time*; the kind who religiously hung towels neatly over the rack or slovenly tossed them over *any which way* (the floor was such a hellish option as not to be considered); the kind who ironed a shirt the proper way or *slap-dashed* through it. There was no doubt, in my grandmother's mind, of which kind of person you wanted to be—and no doubt in ours that our actions were being watched and our character judged at all times. This kind of opprobrium is oppressive, without a doubt, but it's indelible if you've grown up with it. (Even to-day, I could no more leave the house without making my bed than I could walk out the door naked.) The question is: Do you honestly want to foist your neuroses upon another generation? Sure, it's great to be neat but it's also great *not* to be "an anal-retentive maniac" as my step kids and daughter like to characterize me.

When you've got a lot of psychic baggage that you know is interfering with your ability to choose your battles with your teen, try to unload some of that weight. It's not necessary or possible to jettison all your stuff, but most parental ideals are not an all-or-nothing choice. If your kids ultimately adopt 50 percent of your "neurotic obsessions," that might be a step in the correct evolutionary direction.

A fabulous reassurance in this paring-down-to-the-essentials process is the theory that whatever you needed to teach them, you already have. According to this line of reasoning, by the time they become teenagers and certainly by the age of 16 or 17, children have long since finished learning from you, though you won't be able to see the fruits of your labor for a few years, possibly decades. Hopefully you'll like what you see at that point, even if it does bear a frightening resemblance to you.

As arduous as it is to choose your battles, you also need to choose your battlefields. This is a matter of self-discipline and restraint: two things that are not exactly my forte. I can tell you from painful experience that choosing *where* you will allow conflict can either diminish its impact or escalate the bejeezus out of a minor fracas. The following "Quick Guide to Conflict Zones" is my bottom line:

Dinner table	No	*The minute she walks through the door*	No
Watching a beloved TV show	No	*In front of his friends*	No
In their room	No	*In front of your friends*	No
In a neutral area like the hallway	Yes	*In front of siblings*	No
In the car	Maybe	*With your mate*	Yes
Outside (if people aren't around)	Yes		

Notice that there are a lot more No's than Yes's. This is a tiny clue that battles are not something to enter into lightly or unadvisedly (as with marriage).

Make no mistake; choosing your battles is a lot of work and there will be many times when you'll complain to yourself, *"But the way she holds her pen renders her almost completely unable to write and how the hell is she going to get through life like that? Can't I fight about that . . . please?"* And your wise self will answer, *"No. Put a sock in it, Mom!"*

Sure, it sucks to have to compromise your principles on a daily basis. But take comfort in knowing that your child will then be presented with a consistent articulation of your core values that she can digest. Not an undifferentiated mountain of advice you've thrown up, apparently to block any chance of her happiness.

Edit your angst.

You Really Can't Make Them Do Anything

I hate this reality bite and didn't want to include it, but it's my mission to tell the unvarnished truth. This is the elephant in the room that we (our teens *and* us) pretend we don't see because the entire hierarchy of authority depends on everyone buying into the fiction that parents have control. The fact is, once you can no longer pick your kid up and sling him over your shoulder, you cannot force him to do what you say.

The first indication of the tenuousness of your power will doubtless occur to you far earlier than it does to your child, particularly if you have a son. Boys tend to test the waters of parental authority in a far more serious and intentional way than girls. At about age 13, your son will suddenly refuse to do something you've told him he must do and he has previously meekly accepted, like go to church. You reply calmly, "You have to go to church. End of discussion." But to yourself you're thinking, "Damn! What if he won't go? *What the hell am I going to do—drag him to the car and haul him up the church steps?*"

You think back to when you were a teenager and rack your brain for memories of similar patterns of defiance. Unfortunately, there is nothing in your memory bank to support you in your current crisis. It never once occurred to you to openly defy your parents because they probably would have slapped you upside the head merely for expressing a desire to disobey them. Those were the good old days. Now, with nothing in your arsenal of enforcement but a couple of mealy-mouthed threats of grounding and cell phone removal, you're in a no-man's land. You hope with all your might that your teen hasn't realized that you can't physically make her go to school, do her homework, pick up her room, or brush her teeth. You feel powerless and exposed; the emperor has no clothes!

Take five steps back from the abyss and promise yourself never to look over that ledge again. Despite the fact that you know differently, you must behave as if you hold all the cards in this showdown. Fake it if you must. But even to yourself, do not admit that you ultimately have no way to enforce the rules.

This is deadly serious. If you do not believe your teen has to do what you say, there is no way on earth that he's going to buy into that concept. And once you let go of the reins of authority, you will not be able to get them back, short of going through a harrowing tough-love, boot-camp intervention. I'm not advocating that you maintain parental authority to shore up your power-hungry ego or to win some superficial control contest; it's far easier to become your teen's "friend" and take a laissez-faire attitude about whatever he does.

No, you must maintain your authority because it's in your child's best interests that you do. Teens' safety and well-being

absolutely depend on having structure, restrictions, expectations, and the threat of unpleasant consequences surrounding
them. These are the four sacred walls that protect them from
the harsher elements of adult life, and they stand only with
your authority. Sure, teens will challenge you, run their heads
directly into those walls, and often refuse to acknowledge the
walls are there. But the structure will hold. Remind them they
have to do what you say because they are still living under
your roof, you are paying their bills, and you know better
than they do what is in their best interests. Take this aura of
power to the bargaining table with you, and feel your backbone solidify. Become the awesome "She Who Must Be
Obeyed," as my friend Rusty lovingly refers to his spouse.

In today's world of kids indulged beyond anything previously believed possible, this may seem to be totalitarianism
on a grand scale. I'm okay with that. You go, Dictator Mom or
Dad!

How I Changed
My Mind About Consistency

If your parenting skills are as dubious as mine, it's likely you
have the same issues with consistency as I do. Consistency is
universally regarded as the *sine qua non* of good parenting,
and I totally get that. It's important to be firm, logical, and
consistent so children understand the rules and values of the
household and know what is expected of them. Consistency
is the grout that holds the four sacred walls of authority together. If you're constantly changing your mind about what is
and isn't allowed, there is no firm ground on which your
teenager can stand to try to knock those walls down.

TALES FROM POST-TEENS ● ● ● ● ● ● ● ●

The worst thing I remember doing as a teen was when I said I was spending the night at a friend's house and instead I drove down to the beach with a bunch of friends, in the summer after my freshman year of high school. I ended up getting very drunk, having some guy drop me on my head in the sand, and coming home covered in puke and sand the next morning. Nothing good came of those nights when I lied about where I was, with very few exceptions. I feel extremely lucky that I got through those years without more serious consequences. I think the fact that my parents were always looking over my shoulder and "harassing" me—at the same time that they were giving me enough room to make mistakes and learn from them—was what kept me from going completely off the deep end.

But consistency can also be a trap and a great inhibitor to effective negotiation. If your teen believes that you have already made every decision in advance and those decisions are carved in stone, there is no point in bargaining. Teens need to feel they have some input and impact on decisions being made, especially as they get older. Your teen has to have a bit of room to wiggle, to protest, and to try to change your mind. Otherwise, he'll be like a kettle on full boil, with no place for that steam to go, until the lid blows clean off.

Now, it's completely natural to clutch at consistency as if it's a GPS, there to guide you through the confusion and gloom of an unending series of decisions about what you will and won't allow your teens to do. On a daily basis, exhausted parents are asked to render a series of snap judgments that would make

Judge Judy's head spin off. Many times there is no clear answer; you will be swimming in ambivalence, trying to appear decisive while fifty options race through your head. The worst of these decision-making meltdowns happen over the phone, when you're supposed to give an answer to your child in under two seconds . . . *"before you waste all my minutes, Dad!"*

In that whirlwind, you not only feel pressured but you're fairly certain that one wrong decision could be the complete undoing of your kid. Take a deep, cleansing breath, go back to the safety standards, and let those be your guide. Envision yourself as solid and strong, yet flexible. Channel your inner bamboo.

Fact is, it's more important that you make *a* decision—any decision—and your teen generally abides by it, than that every decision has to be consistent or "right." Consistency is great when it comes to the overarching principles you hold dear, but it's wise not to become overly dependent on the status quo. My sister taught me how powerful it can be to surprise your teens by saying yes, particularly in front of their friends, whom they've convinced you are a tyrant on the scale of Genghis Khan. Your unexpected acquiescence may totally throw them off their resentment game.

Over the years, the walls of authority should become more like room dividers. They're still standing firmly in place, but you and your teen can move them around for better effect. It's like Extreme Parenting Makeover.

THE VOICES IN YOUR HEAD ARE RIGHT . . . NO, THEY'RE NOT!

One of the many things that make parenting a teen such an exercise in humility is that you are never sure *what* you are doing, even though you are completely convinced you're not doing it properly. This insecurity is vastly complicated by the fact that at any given time, there are at least two—possibly many more—voices in your head telling you how you should be making decisions regarding your teen. These voices emanate from a variety of sources: your best friend, your sister, Dr. Phil, Dr. Spock, or the most powerful voice of all—your own parents. To get a handle on the cacophony, try to unbraid the thick strand of messages that are whipping through your brain like an electrical wire in the throes of some hideous power surge and identify the competing core messages. Here are a few of mine, touched off by a smattering of Cs on Lulu's past report card:

THE PARENT-AS-FRIEND VOICE:
Betty, your relationship with your daughter is what's most important, not what she is achieving in school. You need to stay close to her—and that's impossible if you're constantly demanding and critical.

THE DARE VOICE:
Don't be a friend. Be a parent.

THE CONSEQUENCES VOICE:
Let her suffer the consequences of her actions. If she does poorly in school, she is only hurting herself and she is the one who has to live with that.

THE RETALIATION VOICE:
You want consequences? I'll give you consequences. She's not going out of this house until she pulls her grades up.

THE PITHY POSITIVE VOICE:
At the end of the day, A students will be the professors, B students will be the managers, and C students will run the world.

THE RESCUER VOICE:
What if her grades keep getting worse and worse? I can't just sit back and let her fail when her whole future is at stake!

THE VICTIM VOICE:
Why is she doing this to me? Why can't she just get good grades and stop torturing me?

THE AA VOICE:
Let go and let God.

THE A VOICE:
God, I need a cocktail.

How do you create any consensus of opinion amidst all these conflicting voices? Quite simply, you can't. When you've got this kind of Greek chorus going on in your brain, it can drive you to exhibit the multiple personalities of Sybil, careening wildly from one parenting approach to the next. Over salad, you may be channeling the Parent-as-Friend; during the main course, the DARE representative; and by dessert, the Retaliation drill sergeant.

I can assure you from bitter experience, this is not effective parenting and will confuse your teen *and* enable him to work you over like Rocky Balboa. From the time your child figured out that you'd pick him up from his crib if he cried hysterically for precisely two and a half minutes, he's known how to get his way with you. That's the nature of the parent/child bond. Given the stakes now, it's only natural he's going to use those skills to best effect. He will know precisely how to stimulate the appearance of each of your multiple personalities, then pit them against each other until you're utterly exhausted and willing to give up on the issue altogether. If you find yourself pitching madly from rage to guilt to remorse in a single evening's conflict with your teen, you can be pretty sure you're being manipulated. (This is completely normal, although not to be recommended.)

It's time to retreat from the fray, collect your thoughts, and get some perspective on what it is that you believe about the situation *at hand*—then construct a plan and implement it. Trying to arrive at a global solution or decide if your plan is universally fair is too much baggage to check at this time. In other words, you don't have to come down hard on the side of any one of your Inner Voices. If you remove the burden of trying to pick The Perfect Path, finding a practical answer to immediate issues will come a lot easier. Give yourself permission to try something for a while, see if it works, and then (particularly if you're visited by Social Services) reexamine the solution.

11

HURDLES ON THE
TRACK TO CONSENSUS

IN ANY NEGOTIATION, IF SOMEONE ACROSS THE TABLE
says "Trust me," that is an excellent indicator that you
shouldn't. That goes triple if the person across the table
from you is a teen. Of course, teens are far too slick to ask
you to trust them outright; they know the best offense is a
good guilt trip. So they're likely to choke out, with extreme
bitterness, some version of: *You just don't trust me!*" The
best renditions of this phrase are heart-rending portraits of
obliterated self-esteem and injured pride. For some reason,
the most impassioned versions come as a result of being
caught red-handed in the very act of untrustworthiness—
which of course the offended teen wouldn't have been
caught in at all if her horrid parents trusted her and didn't
try to entrap her!

As a rule, the dialogue teens will use to bolster their demands at the negotiating table is ridiculous, and you should know that going in. Here are a few of my favorites with the appropriate Bionic Parent response:

> *Nobody else's parents give their teen a curfew.* I'm not giving you a curfew. I'm telling you what time you have to be home.

> *Nobody else's parents check to see if the parents are going to be home.* I guess they don't love their kids as much as I love you.

> *You don't trust me.* Count on it.

The one thing you don't want to take into negotiation is an inclination to buy your teen's bullshit. Giving your teenager your complete trust is like leaving your broker alone with your checkbook. Temptation is everywhere but there's no need for you to lead your teenager into it. Even if your child is impervious to evil (sure), his or her friends will take advantage of the situation you've served up. Remove the temptation. Take the chocolate cake out of reach of the 3-year-old. When you present teens with an irresistible opportunity to do something illicit, who is the numbskull?

Take this advice from my husband and myself (Dumb and Dumber), who used to leave my 17-year-old stepson home alone on weekends while we took the younger kids away. Every Sunday, we'd return to find windows broken, bras festooning the bushes, and kitchen faucets snapped in two. To this day, my husband continues to insist it was the physics professors living behind us who were tossing pink lingerie and beer cans into

TALES FROM POST-TEENS • • • • • • • •

I was 15 and madly in love but my parents wouldn't let me date more than once a week. So I decided to sneak out to meet my boyfriend late one night after babysitting. I had the unwitting parents drop me off at the wrong house and then I snuck around back, met my boyfriend, and was making out like crazy when I glanced up from the bushes to see every light in my house go blazing on, and the babysitting parents screech up to the house. Busted! I had absolutely no justification or excuse, but I remember being completely outraged that my parents had tried to check up on me. How dare they not trust me!

our yard. My stepson, now 26, will shrug and say, "I can't believe that you guys kept going away and leaving me home to throw parties all weekend. What were you thinking?"

Apparently, we weren't thinking. We were *trusting*.

CUTTING OFF YOUR NOSE TO SPITE YOUR FACE AND OTHER UNATTRACTIVE TEEN TRAITS

In negotiation, you expect the people across the table to operate in their own self-interest. You're willing to give up some things to get what you consider to be most important, and you assume the other participants are operating on the same rational playing field. But you are not dealing with anybody rational; you're dealing with a teenager. And that changes everything.

AGONIZING EXAMPLE

At the last minute, Kevin's friend called and offered him tickets to the concert of some gangster rapper he adores. It was a school night, and Kevin's mom, Sarah, hated everything about the idea because he'd be out until midnight and have no time to do his homework, but she knew how much it meant to him. So Sarah agreed that Kevin could go if he would do his algebra problems, a task that would take approximately ten minutes if he applied himself. Instead, he argued for thirty minutes that this demand constituted cruel and unusual punishment, that he could do his math in homeroom tomorrow, and that obviously his mom was hell-bent on ruining his life with her insane focus on schoolwork when he could *handle it himself* (all recent test grades to the contrary). Sarah was literally pleading with Kevin to do his math quick and, in desperation, even offered the option of his doing it the minute he got home. Kevin adamantly refused. His friend pulled up to get him for the concert and there on the front porch, Sarah was forced to say he couldn't go.

A teenager will negotiate with you about something he desperately wants, then suddenly, on the verge of complete success, refuse to accept a conditional request that is of absolutely no consequence. This will throw the entire negotiation off track. You will be outraged that you're stretching a mile and he won't budge an inch. Instead of being able to give him what he wants, you'll be forced into a negative stance you never intended to take.

Does it have to be so damn hard? With some oppositional kids, yes. They'd rather lose the battle *and* the war, for what reason I cannot say. I must have a hundred memories of standing outside Lulu's room, pleading with her not to force my hand and make me remove something she considers a bodily organ, like her cell phone. Invariably, the only thing required to prevent the amputation is something as simple as picking up a sock or unlocking her door. But she'd rather die than give in.

I will stomp into the bathroom and beseech my husband, "Why is she doing this? What is she getting out of being so obstinate? She's got everything to lose, nothing to gain, and she still won't give in!" And he'll look up calmly and say, "I have no idea. But she's been doing this exact same thing since she was 2; she's probably not going to stop now."

Of course, I could avoid the fight by not getting sucked into inconsequential power struggles. That might be a good place to start. But I believe that sometimes teens are so into conflict, they'll find a way to start an inferno no matter how damp and inflammable the tinder. Apparently it's quite satisfying to sacrifice a nose if it gives you the opportunity to spite your face. *And* to prove what a total A-hole your parent is.

WHEN DID I BECOME ANITA BRYANT?

At some point, you will become so unnerved by your teenager's rebellious nature, you will overcompensate and become the lunatic conservative you spent your college years protesting against. Suddenly, out of your mouth will fly sentiments like "The only thing that matters in life is the kind of job you have." "A lady always sits with her knees firmly pressed together." And my personal favorite: "Anybody who drinks or smokes marijuana is a total loser"—no doubt delivered emphatically with a thirty-six-ounce glass of wine in my hand.

It's going to happen. You will get so riled up by your teen-ager's antics, you'll find yourself telling the biggest whoppers of all time. You'll espouse stuff you don't begin to believe but that still might prove to be a compelling argument, or that at least serves as an effective counterweight in your offspring's downward spiral. This is part of the natural order of parent-ing called the Pendulum Effect. Despite the limitations of the results you can expect from the Effect, it's probably a univer-sal inclination in human psychology to attempt to counter-balance extreme behavior.

Thus, when your child pierces her cheek with a steel stud, you will mysteriously find yourself in Talbot's buying multiple twin-sets and strings of pearls, even though you formerly lived in True Religion jeans and cute little bodice-hugging tops. Your son begins to wear ultra-saggy sweats and stocking caps, and you don a pair of nautical topsiders and khakis. Your teens shave their heads, and you start tying your sweater around your neck in that Polo way. And you don't even *like* sweaters!

Think of this dynamic as a seesaw. The further out your teens move toward one end of the fulcrum, the more you're going to feel compelled to push back the other way. You know from years spent on the playground that if you don't compensate for your playmate's extreme movements, it's im-possible to achieve any kind of balance. Of course, it's useful to remember one more important thing about seesaws, which makes them such a mysterious choice as children's equip-ment: The other person can simply decide to hop off when they've had enough and you'll come crashing down on your coccyx. Thus, when your teen abruptly decides he wants something in life and is ready to work for it, he'll suddenly lose the punk look, take off the stocking cap, and switch wardrobes. And you'll still be out there with that dumb striped sweater tied jauntily around your neck.

To thine own self remain true.

If the stresses of raising a teen have completely obliterated your self-awareness and you feel the urge to change everything about yourself to compensate for your offspring's antisocial behavior, resist the urge. Call a friend and plan your own intervention. Give away the clothes that make you feel like a prairie wife. Do not shop alone. And monitor the crap that is flowing out of your mouth like water gushing from a garden hose. Perhaps if your teen sees that you are not the opposite of him and that you, too, once had a rebellious streak a mile wide and suffered through bizarre wardrobe choices, academic misfires, and inappropriate romantic liaisons, he would feel a little less alone. He might even come to trust your advice—but let's not get too Pollyanna here.

Keep your leather pants on and let the chips fall where they may.

THE FEAR OF
THINKING TOO MUCH

It's difficult to negotiate anything when you're operating out of fear. But fear in all its guises is a parent's closest companion.

There is Fear of the Unknown: specifically, fear for the future of your child who seems unprepared for marching band, not to mention real life, as well as fear of what your life will be like when you don't have a child to worry about and take care of anymore. There is Fear of Failure—looming large ever since your teenager barfed Jagermeister all over the assistant principal at last year's homecoming game and you've been getting a lot of "So *that's* the slacker mom responsible" looks from other parents. Likewise, there is Fear of Incompetence, which assails you every time you're called on to make a decision about what to do with your teen. Let him sleep until noon or wake his lazy ass up? Allow her to watch another three episodes of *Fresh Prince of Bel Air* or make her go outside and get some real air? Nag him to pick up the ankle-deep dirty clothes carpeting his bedroom floor or shut the door on the chaos? You have no idea which choice to make! Finally, there is Fear of Fear itself. You've read enough self-help books to know that life will manifest what you focus on—and you suspect that, by wallowing in fear, you're attracting the very things you dread. Yet you can't seem to wean yourself off the relentless worry. It's a classic Catch–22.

Of course, we're not unsupported in our Boomer obsession with fear. The media bombards us daily with stories of car crashes, kidnappings, drive-by shootings, girls disappearing on school trips to Aruba, middle school meth labs, and friends with benefits. Small wonder we're all basket cases.

The problem with fear is that it tends to paralyze you at the exact time you need to be nimble so you can outmaneuver your teen. In the end, a lot of decisions you're required to make aren't going to matter much, one way or another. But when you're laboring under the delusion that you still have a lot of input into your teen's character, every situation seems freighted with utmost importance and clogged with the fear that you'll make the wrong choice.

I call this tendency (of which I am a master) the Trajectory of Catastrophic Thinking.

I'm convinced that the Trajectory of Catastrophic Thinking is actually a clever way for us to overcompensate for our teens' refusal to consider *anything* a problem. A 16-year-old's reluctance to perform his required duties (which is completely normal adolescent behavior, unfortunately) is probably not a sign of impending crisis. It merely means you need to nudge, cajole, and bug him to perform those duties. Try not to fall into the trap of becoming fixated on the potential long-term consequences of your teen's behavior—in direct

AGONIZING EXAMPLE

Square one: Your son forgets his math book several times a week and can't seem to get it together to do his homework. You begin to think about what you can do to rectify the situation, like enlisting the help of his teacher to check that he's got his assignment written down and his book in hand before he leaves school.

Then you start to wonder if his not bringing his book home indicates he is harboring an unconscious desire to fail. You can't understand why he says he hates his teacher when she seems perfectly nice to you. Perhaps he's having problems with interpersonal skills and authority figures, which of course would be linked to his desire to fail.

At this point, your thoughts begin to cascade and pick up real steam. He didn't do well in math last year and maybe he's losing confidence in academics altogether. You probably shouldn't have kept him in this school when clearly he's much more artistic than linear in his thinking and he's probably not being supported or taught in the way he can learn. In fact, the pressure of this school is probably turning him off to any kind of intellectual life forever! If only you hadn't switched him from Montessori into that rigid kindergarten when he was 4, maybe he would still be imaginative, engaged, and filled with a love of learning, instead of being listless and bored in ninth grade. And maybe if you wake up every night at 4 A.M. and obsess about every one of these issues, things will really improve with your child.

Or not.

proportion to his total lack of interest in those consequences. This is a huge waste of your time and a squandering of energy. More important, it inhibits him from owning his problems and makes you responsible for everything.

Instead of allowing your mind to run wild, try to focus on the *immediate and direct* solution to the problem at hand. In the above example, you were doing fine with contacting the teacher and setting up a plan of action to support the homework cause. Quit there. When you find yourself tempted to think globally about all the things that could possibly go wrong with your teen, stop the tragedy train in its tracks. Think ahead no more than a week and continue to message to your teen that he needs to do what he needs to do.

Take a chill pill.

HALF-ASSEDNESS

This hurdle to successful negotiation is bound to hit you where it hurts. Because even after you slog through conflict and reach consensus, there is no guarantee that your teen will follow through on his end of the bargain.

As an adult, you are continually required to do things that you don't want to do, like attending pointless meetings and putting out the garbage. These things can be deeply annoying and interrupt the life of leisure you were hoping to lead. But do them you must. This is called maturity. Unfortunately, your teen may not yet have fully bought into the necessity of completing unpleasant tasks he agreed to do, or even starting them. And this half-assed attitude is likely to piss you off.

It will enrage you because it was part of the bargain you struck, and by not following through, your teen is breaking the contract. You had to do a considerable number of chores

AGONIZING EXAMPLE

A woman in my health club told me that her 14-year-old son called her at work to ask her how to open a roll of paper towels. Instead of telling him to read the manual (my snotty retort to brain-dead teen "questions" that are only meant to make you do it for them), she explained how to tear the plastic off and look for the end of the roll. Her son heaved a mighty sigh and said, "Oh forget it. It's too hard. At moments like these, mandatory military service begins to seem like an excellent option."

growing up, none of which you've similarly demanded of your kid. Instead of being grateful for this gigantic pass, teens resent being asked to do anything. And when asked, they'll screw the job up completely so that presumably, you'll learn your lesson and never require them to help out again.

If you want to give yourself a total anxiety attack, read the little book *1001 Things Every Teen Should Know Before They Leave Home (Or Else They'll Come Back)*. I wanted to run directly to school, pull Lulu out of class, and begin home-schooling her in domestic tasks for the final eighteen months of high school. Then I realized that my husband, the university president, is similarly ruled by a "get it done by somebody else" mentality and he's been able to live the fantasy. (Great enabling tip: Marry a girl from a gigantic Irish Catholic family. We're like work horses.)

So, is half-assedness a state of transition that every teen must pass through, like Delaware, or is it, God forbid, a destination? I guess that depends on the teenager. In any event, there's only so much you can do to advance the development of competence.

When you see your teen handling tasks in a half-assed way, point it out and insist that he do it right. But try not to panic or to get too worked up over it. Far better to say, "Do it over and do it right." Then walk away. (Of course, it's far, far easier to do the stupid task yourself, but we all know where that dark path leads.)

THE MYTH OF PARENTAL SOLIDARITY

The teen years are what separate the lions from the lambs, the wheat from the chaff, and the sharks from the amoebas. In other words, this era is what separates parents with spines from those who are sadly without. It's good to know this going in so you don't get your hopes up in the spectacularly disappointing quest for Universal Parental Solidarity at the negotiating table.

Unless you happen to stumble into a social network of protective, strict, and unwavering parents (move to Utah!), you're likely to encounter a lot of weenie parents out there—whose kids just happen to be friends with yours. Parents who serve alcohol to teens in high school because they'd rather have them get drunk at home. Parents who buy into unalloyed crap like coed slumber parties for middle schoolers because "Everybody is doing it and the kids love it." (So what? Kids love to pull down each other's pants and grope each other, too, but that doesn't mean you provide a nice, dark place for them to do it.) And parents who know your kid is doing something dangerous or illegal but won't tell you because they told their child they wouldn't spill the beans and they don't want to violate that "trust."

Parents like these are a mystery—one that you shouldn't spend two seconds trying to solve. Or resolve. Simply get away from them as quickly as possible. Spend your time promoting your teen's friendships with kids whose parents call to see if you will be home when there's a party at your house. Parents who show up promptly when their kid is supposed to be picked up. And parents who don't intervene on behalf of the teens and try to talk you into some half-baked scheme that you know will end badly.

Trust your own instincts and do not stretch beyond the limits you're comfortable with, trying to be like other parents. "But everybody else is letting their kid do it" sounds eerily similar to the teenager's classic and unconvincing "But all the other kids are doing it." Don't go there. Lead by example and let other parents mimic you. It's sort of a backhanded compliment, but I've heard many a teenager in the backseat of my car, bragging about how strict their parents are and one-upping each other with stories of the atrocities of oppression they suffer. Parents who try to ingratiate themselves with teenagers by being lax will be used voraciously and held in utter contempt. Teens are dumb but they're not stupid. The favorite parents are the ones who have lots of food in the house, are open to kids coming over, and have easy-going ways but don't let anyone get away with crap.

You never know how many other parents are out there, waiting for one brave Mom & Dad to lay down the law with their teenager and show everyone else that it's okay to have rules. I'm always grateful for the parent who calls with trepidation to "check in." My response is an automatic "Oh, another maniac of overprotection! Welcome!" Every aging Baby Boomer is afraid of looking uncool, or embodying the dreaded helicopter parent.

Well, I like to think of myself as a Black Hawk. And I am not going down.

12

How to Quid-Pro-Quo
Like a Pro

STEP ONE: DON'T TAKE THEM TOO SERIOUSLY.

If you're going to negotiate successfully with a teenager, you need to develop a thick skin—approximately the depth of an elephant's hide. This will protect you from the inevitable onslaught of attacks on your personality, your looks, and your meager accomplishments. It will also deflect the litany of your teenager's complaints about her life that, were you to take them seriously, might convince you that she should be hospitalized, or perhaps even starring in *General Hospital*. Here are some of my favorites from the Agony archives.

I hate my room.

I hate our TV.

I hate our computer.

I hate this house.

I hate our car.

I hate our neighborhood.

I hate this town.

I hate this city.

I hate this state.

I hate this world.

I want to go to school in Tanzania.

I want to save the whales in Alaska.

I want to join the Navy.

I want to skip college and live on a commune in Idaho.

I want to move to L.A. and be a rock star.

I want my own apartment.

I want to move in with my girlfriend's family.

I'm bored.

I'm sick.

I'm starving.

I'm depressed.

I have no friends.

I want to quit high school.

I want to quit college.

I want to delay going to college for a year.

I want to delay going to college for a decade.

I want you to give me all the money you would have spent on college.

I want you to give me all the money you'd give me if you died.

APPROPRIATE PARENTAL
RESPONSE TO ALL OF THE ABOVE

Good to know.

The idea is not to respond to any statement that doesn't have action behind it. It's a total waste of time. Validate the concept and watch how quickly that deadens your teens' enthusiasm. Do not engage in speculative dissing of their ideas. You've got enough real stuff to argue about; you certainly don't need to bring imaginary combatants into the ring. Instead, embrace what they say. Co-opting a disruptive or revolutionary idea is a time-honored capitalistic trick that you can use to your own advantage. (Think of how quickly corporate America embraced rap to sell beer and blue jeans.)

As long as there is no action, threats are not a threat.* This is not to belittle the trial balloons your teen is floating up to see what feels right, or the potential lifestyles he's adopting to figure out who he is. It means when teens are ranting to provoke a reaction from you, don't give them the satisfaction. You don't have to shoot down their flights of fancy or point out the impossibility of their precocious ideas; time will take care of that. If and when those ephemeral concepts become a reality, you can figure out how to respond. But right now, they're only clouds in the sky. Lie back and watch them pass by.

*Obviously, I'm not talking about real threats of suicide or violence that must be taken seriously, with therapists consulted. As a parent you should know if your child is a danger to him- or herself or others and take appropriate action. My advice is meant for the 45 million kids who are a threat only to their parents' sanity.

MOVE TO THE SOLUTION

This is such an adult concept, it's almost R-rated. But it's the very bedrock of streamlined negotiation.

Teenagers love to stay mired in the problem. They love to discuss it, bemoan it, freak out about it, rant about it, and resent it. The one thing they are loath to do is figure out a way to solve it. Take the typical teen reaction to getting a crap grade at school. Mitigating circumstances he will love to explore include: the teacher is mean, the textbook got lost, the grading was unfair, the other students were loud, the homework wasn't assigned, the quiz was popped, the questions were confusing, the pencil was broken, the study guide was flawed, and the essay was brutal. Exploring the problem is staying in the swamp. Moving to the solution (*get a tutor!*) is your exit strategy.

Deal with what *is*. Then figure out a plan to get where you want to go. And drag your teenager behind you, kicking and screaming, on the road to the solution.

Exploring all the ramifications, mysteries, and contingencies of the problem won't get you any closer to solving it. It often takes awhile for me to grasp this myself, as there is a weird satisfaction in thrashing around in the muck and bitch, bitch, bitching about the problem. It can take an almost physical effort to pick yourself up and move to higher ground where suddenly, a solution will present itself. Voilà!

Envision yourself at 20,000 feet looking down at the situation. Go for the big picture. Get some perspective. Find your way out of the forest *and* the trees.

(The above clichés are suitable for copying on Post-its and slapping all over your teenager's room. Enjoy!)

They Don't Have to Like You

Newsflash: Not only do teens not have to like you, they're not even *supposed* to like you. Right now, it's our teens' job to snap the strong cords that still bind them to us so they can grow up and move away. In fact, you are raining on their pity parade if you so much as attempt to ameliorate the situation.

Remember when you were a teen, how great it felt to disavow that you were even *related* to your family? Remember how you held in contempt every curtain in your house, the creepy carpet, and the hideous furniture? I actually wrote a

AGONIZING EXAMPLE

Ted's son Nick had to finish a paper for history class. Nick had typed the paper on his computer in the basement, which was residing there because his Dell had been removed from his bedroom the week before in response to an email grenade from his Spanish teacher about missing homework. Unfortunately, that move disconnected Nick from the Internet (bonus) and severed his connection to the wireless printer (oops!). At eleven o'clock at night, after several hours spent video-gaming and in other non-homework-related pursuits, Nick discovered he had no way to print out his paper or send it to another computer. Ted spent thirty minutes moving Nick's computer back up to his room and made numerous unsuccessful attempts to reconnect him to the Internet and printer, while Nick fumed at the atrocity of his parents having molested his computer.

"When you are so worried about my grades, Dad, I think it's *ironic* that you would do something that would actually *prevent* me from doing my homework!" he complained.

Ted was quite impressed with Nick's grasp of the complexities of irony but mostly, he was moving to the solution. The assigned paper was short and it suddenly occurred to Ted that in five minutes, he could retype it on his own laptop and print it out from there. Ted went happily up to Nick's bedroom, where Nick was lying morosely on his bed. Ted presented his neat solution, and his laptop, with a flourish. Nick would have none of it. Instead, he spent the next hour trying to get his old printer to work, adding print cartridges, lobbing a few swears in Ted's direction, and staying firmly mired in the problem. Ted wanted to strangle his son. Instead, he left his laptop outside Nick's door and went to bed.

short story for my high school literary magazine on the mundane, middle-class tackiness of my suburban home—and did my parents care one iota? Nope. Did they then redecorate to try to make our home more appealing to me? Sure they did—and then they set up a space station for my siblings and me so we'd be more comfortable on our own *planet*.

But today, everything is different. We can't stand our kids to be discontent, and so we deny them the exit strategy that worked so well for us. Our kids literally have nothing to reject. In our frantic desire to prevent them from experiencing five consecutive minutes of unhappiness we've already removed every obstacle in their path. And how unrealistic is that? Life has many, many moments (even years) of unhappiness in store for each of us, and part of growing up is learning how to deal with disappointment, setbacks, and failure. By not allowing our teens to have anything to despise and reject, we're depriving them of their inalienable right to be alienated from us . . . what a shame!

A more enlightened way to approach negotiation with your teen is to concentrate on doing what you feel is in your kid's best interests, and callously blowing off how your child is going to "feel" about the decision. (Exactly like your parents, and their parents, did before.) This is not only liberating, it's incredibly effective. The next time you feel an underlying desperate need for a negotiation with your teen to conclude with him liking you, try this. Imagine the United Auto Workers in negotiation with GM, thinking that not only do they need to extract pension, benefits, and salary concessions from the corporation, but they're not getting up from the table until they get a big, heartfelt hug." OK with you?

Wean yourself off the fantasy of a happy ending. Embrace the beauty of grudging respect.

Agonizing Example

Last year, my friend Gabrielle had a wrenching argument with her 17-year-old about getting the new Xbox. The fight became horribly bitter, as Caleb felt his mom's unwillingness to buy it represented her "tyrannical" desire to deprive him of every worldly pleasure and ruin his life. For two solid weeks, almost without respite, he yelled and nagged at Gabrielle from the moment he got home until he went to bed. Then one day she simply stopped arguing the pros and cons of the Xbox and said, "Caleb, absolutely not. It's never going to happen." The minute he realized the discussion was truly over, he shrugged, fired off one final "I hate you," and dropped the whole thing. Gabby was stupefied that he accepted her edict and wondered why the hell she'd wasted two weeks trying to placate, convince, and persuade him, when all she had to do was end it with a firm "No."

Your Secret Weapon:
A Mother's Intuition

I'm not saying dads don't have it. Plenty of them do, I'm sure, and John Irving novels prove it. But there is something about mothers being so keenly attuned to their children's safety that allows us to sense when something is not right in a given situation. I've heard the same story countless times, about mothers who were just at the point of giving in and letting their child do something when some sixth sense told them not to do it. Sometimes all that was averted was a scary walk through a bad neighborhood at midnight; and sometimes it was a party that spun wildly out of control. Fact is, you *do* have intuition about what you should and shouldn't allow your teen to do, and you should definitely honor it. When something makes you feel physically uncomfortable—anxious, prickly, and hyper-skeptical about what your teen is telling you—then either get more information or say no.

Teens aren't very subtle, and they give a lot of signals that will tip you off if you're paying attention. Don't bargain away your power of intuition.

Trust yourself. You're smarter than you think.

TRY A LITTLE TENDERNESS

My daughter would burst out laughing if she read this, because I can be a pretty harsh parent when it comes to certain things like grades and cleanliness. But I think you do have to allow your kids to make mistakes and forgive them for their transgressions. Very few kids will get through their teen years without doing something so patently dumb and infuriating that it takes away your power of speech (and possibly their license). As I mentioned before, teens are prone to lie, sneak, make poor decisions, and possibly drink, do drugs, and have sex long before you think they should. And you will have to love and accept them in spite of it.

What's the alternative: kicking them out of your life? What would that accomplish besides breaking your heart in two? It's far more likely that, when your child does something idiotic or pulls away from you entirely, she needs you the most. This is not to say that you shouldn't have rules, curfews, high expectations, and consequences for your child. But when your teen screws up, you don't have to make a federal case out of it. You can treat them like they screwed up, establish a consequence, and move on.

I realize some transgressions are more serious than others, but save the zero tolerance for things that are truly life threatening. I've known a lot of parents who drug-test their kids, because they are convinced that marijuana is such a powerfully negative influence. As long as it's done in a reasonable, respectful way (try to avoid the technique of the dad in *American Beauty*), and with carefully spelled-out consequences, I think that's fine. Just keep in mind that buying clean urine is simpler than you might imagine. (Can you spell *craigslist*?)

But when you find yourself being harsh for no viable reason, or relentlessly harping on past bad behavior, your relationship can become nothing more than a battle for control. This situation your teen will instantly recognize and fight to the death to win. In any negotiation, if the *only* answer for why you're intent upon getting your teen to do or not do

WORDS OF WISDOM

My friend Ginger is one of eleven children, nine of them big, strapping Irish boys. It goes without saying that her awesome mother Jean has had lots of practice in dealing with kids falling off the straight and narrow path in adolescence. Jean's strategy, which Ginger has adopted with her four teenage girls, is to give each child one freebie-to-screw-up. This means the first (and *only* the first) time a teen goes out and gets drunk, barfs all over the bedroom, or gets in trouble, there is no consequence. There will be a serious conversation, and the infraction is not treated lightly, but trust in the child is not irrevocably broken. (The second screw-up is a whole different story.) Ginger has a great memory and can vividly recall the misdeeds of her own youth. So she's decided not to come down hard on her girls for that first big misdeed, especially when her mom gave her some room to screw up and still be a great kid.

something is "Because I said so," you can be pretty sure that you're being driven by the wrong motivation. Let it go.

One of the things that struck me in the letters from post-teens was the gratitude they almost unanimously expressed about being allowed to screw up and be forgiven. In retrospect they realized they had sorely tested their parents' patience and bank accounts. They felt sorry for their idiotic behavior and surly, unappreciative attitudes, particularly in the face of their parents' unconditional love through all the troubling teen years. Wouldn't it be nice if your teen looked back and felt the same way?

Stage 5: Acceptance

AGE 18,
THE GLADIT'SOVER EPOCH

DESPITE THE DREAD THAT THE TEEN YEARS ARE A nightmare from which you will never awaken, there is an infallible cure for adolescence. It's called time. And just like Mick Jagger promised, it's on your side.

Your teen's adulthood is now so close you can almost reach out and hug it. Consecutive hours go by without a single hysterical outburst or subversive challenge. It's almost disorienting. In fact, some days you don't even feel like exerting your authority except over your partner (who is likely to become the focus of your undivided attention, much to his or her dismay).

As surely as the previous years have been a whirlwind of immediate crises and impending conflicts, the final years (you hope) of your child living at home are consumed with looking forward to and preparing for the future. Where you were once larger than life and twice as annoying, your daughter now barely notices that you're in the room. Your son is so mature, he may even initiate a conversation. Big changes are afoot. There is the dreaded college search. The last homecoming. The SAT, ACT, AP, and WTF. You begin to alter your own behavior, too. You stop stockpiling linens. You don't pick up a new pack of tube socks every time you hit Target. You even figure you might as well buy that adorable little Honda Fit because you won't have as many kids to schlep around anymore. The end is near.

As the long slog of parenting a teenager winds down and your child prepares to move out into the world, a host of bittersweet emotions sweeps over you. No, it probably didn't have to be so hard. Yes, you can let him go and he probably will be okay. And you can rest uneasily, knowing that nothing's entirely finished and your child will forever be your child—driving you crazy, making you proud, and giving you reason to live.

This is the land of Acceptance, a place you thought you would never live to see. A land where you live in the present, not the future or past, and have learned to coexist peacefully with adolescent tattoos, unmade beds, and a stunning lack of ambition. Before you go gentle into that good night, however, there are likely to be a few bumps in the road. Fasten your seat belts. It's not over quite yet.

13

BLINDING FLASHES
OF THE OBVIOUS

I LIKE TO THINK OF ADOLESCENCE AS THE SIX-YEAR
process of landing the space vehicle (also known as your
teenager) and bringing it safely back to earth. Whether the final reentry is smooth and graceful or turbulent as hell, the
initial stage of Acceptance is marked by sudden revelations
about parenting. These are insights that, were you to share
them with any rational person, he or she would look at you
in pity and respond, "Well, no shit, Sherlock." But any ago-
nized parent will understand the beautiful moment when
you're struck by something you intellectually understood but
never truly accepted—like the idea that there is a college out
there that will admit your son. Or the notion that your
daughter might someday pick up the phone and voluntarily
talk to you.

These revelations are profound, yet fleeting. You're almost afraid to believe they're true, and your teen isn't exactly a model of consistency to help you out there. One day he seems ready to run a small country; the next, you wouldn't trust him to brush his own teeth. So you may not fully grasp how far you've come in your parenting journey and all that you've accomplished. The experience of letting your teen go may feel both exhilarating and reprehensible, as if you're throwing in the towel and abandoning your parental responsibilities. It's hard to hold on to enlightenment.

Try to focus on the insights and prolong the nanoseconds of peacefulness. Remind yourself that the darkest hour is just before dawn (or happy hour). Any ups and downs you're experiencing are a natural indicator of how close to the end of this marathon you are. Pat yourself on the back for your remarkable stamina, and expect a few epiphanies along the home stretch.

You Are Not Them / They Are Not You

When your baby is first born, he is tiny and helpless and depends on you for everything. For those of us who need to be needed, these are the glory days. Yet as your child develops the ability to walk, talk, and say *NO!* you begin to understand that your child does not belong to you. He belongs to himself. She is her own ferocious little person.

However, thanks to the genetic bonds you share, you may have a bit more trouble coming to grips with the fact that your child isn't some cuter, younger version of you. You may look at her snub nose and think—just like mine! You observe his tendency to rub his head when he's tired and think—just like me! You may even walk around predicting confidently, "The apple doesn't fall far from the tree!" Small wonder some teens have significant identity-theft issues with their parents.

But as you reluctantly accept the reality that your children are not you, you may come to a stunning parallel conclusion: You are not them! And this truth, brothers and sisters, will set you free.

If your son drops out of high school, he is the one who is going to have to live with the consequences. If your daughter goes behind your back and gets a tattoo, the dove of peace will be on her butt, not yours. And if your twins are crowned king and queen of homecoming, named co-valedictorian, and get into Harvard, it still won't alter the fact that you were horribly unpopular in high school. For better or for worse, it's their life to live, not yours.

As you realize that you are *not* defined by your child's accomplishments or misdeeds, you will experience a new sense of self that is utterly separate and distinct from the parental you. This person doesn't wake up in a cold sweat of anxiety listening for car wheels in the middle of the night; he sleeps like a baby! She's not in an endless sprint of multitasking from dawn to midnight; she selfishly works out, doesn't cook, and lets laundry pile up, willy-nilly! (You may have to reintroduce yourself if you've totally forgotten this person exists.) Concentrating on yourself instead of on your teen causes a chain reaction of positive energy to ripple through your life. You can give your teen room to breathe and grow, even when it's in a bizarre direction. More important, you get to reclaim your own life and start living voraciously, instead of vicariously, before you're too old to have any fun at all.

TALES FROM POST-TEENS ● ● ● ● ● ● ● ● ●

My family is Quaker, and I was raised with a real nonviolent ethic. All the spiders and flies in the house were caught and released outdoors, we had "War Is Not the Answer" bumper stickers plastered all over our car, and my parents didn't want me to play football because it was so "violent." You know the type. Naturally, the minute I got to high school, I decided I wanted to work for the CIA. I studied a couple foreign languages, read everything I could about political science and counterintelligence, and even visited my congressman to learn how to get into the agency. It must have killed them, but my parents didn't say a thing. They just let me oppose everything they believed in and figured I'd come to my senses eventually. After I got to college, the whole idea seemed ridiculous. But I'm sure if my parents had made a big deal out of opposing it, I would probably be working undercover in Moscow right now.

Everything Is Not Possible

With acceptance comes the ability to see your child more clearly. That's the good and the bad news. Because reality may force you to give up a few of the fantasies every parent secretly harbors for the future.

In some ways, the narrowing of possibilities for your child represents your worst fear. You wanted everything for him; now it appears that you're going to have to settle for considerably less. On the other hand, the narrowing of possibilities is inevitable in every life.

For instance, it should be clear by now that you are not going to marry Angelina Jolie or Viggo Mortenson. Bill Gates is not going to demand that you get a shot at the helm of Microsoft. You probably won't learn to fly a jet, fly fish, or fly through the air with the greatest of ease if you haven't already done so. These realities are not tragic; they are a normal result of the choices you've made in life and your own limitations (and of course, your mate's tolerance for extracurricular activities). Same goes for your beloved teenager.

Part of acceptance is learning to love yourself and others for their true essence, not what has been accomplished or accumulated. That means being okay with what is, *and* what never will be. Conversely—or maybe perversely—the traits that you find truly obnoxious and worrisome in your child may be precisely what makes her successful. Take a deep, cleansing breath. And hum to yourself, "Que sera, sera. . . . "

You Can Be Replaced

The minute you start talking about college with your teenager (or perhaps years before), you will realize one incontrovertible truth. You are the least qualified person for the job. And like any good executive, you should replace yourself immediately with someone who can be more effective.

Don't get offended; it has nothing to do with your knowledge, experience, or interest in the college admissions process. You're not fit for the job because you're the parent. This means that your teenager cannot hear a single word you say, due to the *"What do you know?"* factor (which Lulu and my stepkids have used to wrenching effect in discussions about college with my husband, the president of a university). Additionally,

Agonizing Example

My friend Jocelyn has two daughters, one of whom was a sparkling joy in high school, the other a dark, scary mystery. The older daughter was a prom queen and brilliant student who earned a full science scholarship to an elite college. The younger was a shy, awkward misfit who dressed only in black and spent day and night in the basement on the computer, creating an online magazine for punk rockers. Jocelyn totally related to her older daughter but had no idea how to communicate with the younger one, whom she felt was frankly a bit strange. Fast forward. The prom queen ended up giving up her scholarship and the chance for a prestigious internship so she could come back to State U and marry her slacker boyfriend who has been living on permanent disability for the past eight years. The misfit daughter went to a local engineering college and perfected her Web design skills, interned at some of the city's best design firms, then landed a high-paying job in New York with an Internet publishing company that loved her radical perspective.

Jocelyn is confounded, amazed, and bemused by the turn of events, saying, "You just never know how it's all going to shake out."

everything you say is suspect because you have an ulterior motive: You care about the outcome too much.

So, you need to find somebody else who can step in and identify what schools your child should apply to and oversee the process. This might be the school guidance counselor, an education consultant who does such things for a living, or even a friend or relative who's interested in your child and understands the drill. Their neutrality will be a huge boon to your teen and expedite the search, as you won't be spending 90 percent of his application-essay-writing time arguing, threatening, and nagging. Of course, you can still go on college visits, read the admissions application, and weigh in on the final decision. But to save your relationship and your sanity, leave the nuts and bolts of the admissions process to somebody else.

In fact, replacing yourself as college admissions advisor, homework coach, weight counselor, hair consultant, romance therapist, dance instructor, etiquette guide, and financial tutor in your teen's life is a darn good idea. Put yourself out to pasture and see.

A Few Things to Live For

Facing the prospect of the end (you hope) of your child living at home is terribly sad. To cheer you up, I've made a list of all the things you can put behind you, once your kid has gone. Even if you're a total sap (like me), you've got to admit you won't be forlorn to bid this list farewell.

Annoying Parental Tasks You'll Never Have to Do Again

1. Sell Sallee Anne gift wrap to your friends, neighbors, and co-employees.
2. Buy a freezer-full of Girl Scout cookies at $4/box.

3. Bring snacks for soccer.
4. Sit through a gazillion hours of matches, in the rain and freezing cold, on a Sunday.
5. Supervise and enforce religious education.
6. Go to school plays.
7. Go to school musicals.
8. Go to school band concerts.
9. Go to school talent shows.
10. Go to school football games.
11. Go on scout camping trips.
12. Chaperone field trips in which you're the only mean parent.
13. Decorate gyms.
14. Give blood in school drives.
15. Pay for bad school pictures.
16. Pay for retakes of bad school pictures.
17. Pay for lost library books.
18. Shop for dress-up clothes for school dances.
19. Buy teachers' gifts for teachers you can't stand.
20. Look at another report card.
21. Get another call from your kid's teachers.
22. Get another call from the school principal.
23. Have to live through finals.
24. Have to live through prom hysteria.
25. Have to let go.

Ask Not for Whom the Wolf Whistles. . . . For It Is Not You

This last one is a girl thing. And it's not easy to admit.

If you're remotely cute (and you are), you have become accustomed to men giving you the once-over. Construction guys. Corporate suits. Frat boys. From the time you were a teenager, guys have been checking you out.

Then comes The Change—the first time you walk down the street with your daughter and you realize that the guys aren't checking you out; they're lusting after your daughter. Your sex-goddess sun is setting and hers is rising. In one tidal wave of emotion, you simultaneously feel depressed because you've apparently turned into an invisible old hag, thrilled because your daughter is so lovely and desirable, and jealous that she is much hotter than you (except when you have those insane flashes). Above all, the experience is frightening as hell, since your precious daughter is attracting the attention of men old enough to be her *father*, as well as scumbags so extreme you want to jump in front of her and holler, *"In your dreams, pal!"* Chances are, she won't even notice the attention and will be appalled if you point it out to her. Then, like you, she'll take it for granted.

Aging sucks and has very little to recommend it, but it is inevitable. You can either take this opportunity to live in baggy sweat pants and give up trying to look good, or whip yourself back into shape and work on looking your best every time you step out the door. Just please don't do that tarted-up mom thing, wearing wrinkly-cleavage-revealing shirts and low-rider jeans with your stomach hanging out. Nobody wants to see a 50-year-old stomach, as Ellen Barkin famously said, not even a nice flat one.

Instead of pathetically striving to outshine your daughter, bask in her reflected glory. Go buy yourself some excruciatingly expensive face cream and slap it on, while you pretend that you're aging as well as Sophia Loren, Diane Keaton, Jane Fonda, and Susan Sarandon. Believe in the possibility (however minuscule) of beauty at any age. And don't forget: your daughter got her good looks from you.

14

THE BEAUTY
OF PERSPECTIVE

"DISTANCE" IS A MUCH-MALIGNED WORD. BEHIND IT are a thousand miles of bad road: Distancing parents lead directly to years of therapy. Long-distance lovers are totally suspect. And "I think we need a little distance" is a statement most often used as a prelude to divorce. In many relationships, distance is perceived as both threatening and painful. Yet it's often an essential ingredient in your appreciation of a person who drives you crazy on a day-to-day basis.

With teenagers, of course, distance is practically a religion. My stepkids and daughter used to frantically wrestle each other in restaurants to get the seats that didn't put them next to me. It really hurt my feelings, before years of living with teens caused me to lose all sensation in the heart area. By now, you too have probably given up trying to be close to your kids. Even a dense parent can be spurned for only so long before finally giving up the chase.

And then, something wonderful happens. Your teen sort of misses the sensation of you breathing down his neck and seeks out your company even when he doesn't need a ride. Your daughter plops down on the sofa next to you and actually allows your two arms to touch. If teens believe you aren't going to intrude too forcefully into their lives, as they get older, they may voluntarily begin to grant you limited access.

Much as you dread the impending separation, you begin to see there are real benefits in getting some distance from your teen. Improved mental health, parental self-esteem, and sustained bathroom cleanliness are just the beginning. You'll also be able to remember all the things you admire about your kids when they're not around to provoke you into a daily rage.

It may seem like the ultimate irony that your teen has to put some space between you before you can love each other again, but perhaps that's the way it's supposed to work. All I am saying is—give distance a chance. You may begin to see things in a whole new light.

PEAKING IN HIGH SCHOOL AND OTHER PERILS OF PERFECTION

I'm in no danger of suffering from overachievement with our two current teens, so there may be a slight sour-grapes flavor to this advice. But just in case you too are the parent of a slightly-less-than-stellar teenager, I'm here to tell you (and myself) that this may not be such a bad thing.

After all, there is a downside to achieving the high point of your life in high school; Bruce Springsteen wrote "Glory Days" about the perils of this phenomenon.

For parents of the homecoming queen and star quarterback (and especially parents of kids who can't get a date to the prom), it's important to realize that nobody's glory days last forever. In fact, one of the great joys of attending high school reunions is seeing the golden boys and girls who triumphantly reigned over the rest of us reappear as bald, spread-ing, middle-aged bores, while the geeks and ugly ducklings emerge as dynamic achievers with amazing careers and totally hot spouses.

Let's be honest. What is often valued most in high school is conformity, obedience, and a talent for memorization—not exactly qualities likely to vault you to success in the outside world. (In fact, many studies have shown that class valedictorians almost never turn out to be the most accomplished adults in life.) Creativity, risk-taking, original thinking, and irrepressible confidence are what get you ahead in today's business world, but what do these traits look like in a teenager? They're likely to characterize a kid who challenges every rule, does things his own way, and has a proclivity for spending a lot of time in detention.

The trouble with early perfection is that it traps you in that place of success where risk is unthinkable and growth impossible.

If your child is ultra-driven, she may need a bit of guidance to help her figure out what makes her happy and a boatload of support to learn to honor that. You might want to start in high school or earlier to try to lighten the load that your overachiever is carrying. Instead of constantly pushing our kids to succeed so we can be parents of perfect kids, perhaps we should be messaging that the best thing they can do

AGONIZING EXAMPLE

Rachel, a brilliant student driven to perfection, went to Princeton and got her law degree at Yale. She moved to San Francisco in her 20s and has spent the last ten years with a big-time law firm on the partner track, pulling down some serious cash. But Rachel hates her job, has little time to spend with friends, works eighty-hour weeks, and at 32 is desperately lonely. Her mom knows her daughter would love teaching and derive tremendous satisfaction from it, not to mention have a shot at a real life with a husband and kids. But Rachel is so competitive she can't give up her high-status position. She's terrified that without it she'd cease to exist, at least in the eyes of her Yale friends. So for now, she's trapped in a life she's living to impress others.

is find what they love and follow their hearts. Of course we want to be sure our kids have the skills to get ahead, but we also need to teach them how to get a life. Go for it. Have some fun. (If we haven't totally forgotten how to ourselves.)

It always helps to remember that failure won't kill us, and sometimes it's what pushes us where we're supposed to be. At least that's the way it's worked in my life.

OF COURSE THEY'RE GOING TO GET INTO COLLEGE

Acceptance (the stage) is not synonymous or even necessarily compatible with acceptance (into college), although many

AGONIZING EXAMPLE

(The following is an actual description—but fictional name—of a student whose accomplishments were read aloud on Senior Night at the homecoming football game at Lulu's school. After this and a dozen similar recitations, I suspect I was one of many parents in the stands who couldn't wait to get home and give my kid a huge hug. It must be a total nightmare going to school every day with Mr. Perfecto.)

"BILLY BOB DOE: Track, grades 9–12; Basketball, grades 9–12; Student Government Senator, grades 10–12; Senior Class Vice President; President of the Investment Club; Member of the Marching Band and Jazz Band; Peer Leader; Spirit Award; fifth in State in the National Spanish Exam; Honor Council/Discipline Board; National Honors Society; Homecoming Court; Key Club; Friendliest Award; Gold Eagle."

parents are laboring under that misconception. Our society has placed such an insane emphasis on the process of getting into college, it's no wonder many people believe the penultimate accomplishment in life is acceptance into an Ivy League school.

Unfortunately, Acceptance has nothing to do with where your kid goes to college; in fact, I could make a convincing argument that parents' obsession over college is one of most formidable barriers to embracing your child as a unique individual. In the long run, of course, it doesn't make that much difference *where* your child goes to college. Over 90 percent of the CEOs of the Fortune 500 companies did not go to an Ivy League school, and they seem to be making a decent living. Clearly, college is nothing to flip out over.

Yet somehow we Boomers have glommed onto the idea that our kids must be athletically brilliant, musically inclined, academically advanced, creatively gifted, socially adept, unfailingly polite, linguistically accomplished, globally aware paragons of community service and leadership . . . *or they'll never get into college at all*!

Bullshit. As the wife of a university president, I'm here to tell you, colleges need students. In fact, a multibillion-dollar industry has sprung up to help colleges identify, reach, attract, and enroll students. Colleges want students. Students are the raw material without which they cannot function; they are the only reason colleges exist! Why, then, have we parents convinced ourselves that we are in a sellers' market and need to take desperate measures to promote our children to institutions that don't want them, at any price we are willing to pay? (And it's pushing $200,000 right now.)

Beats me. It is not impossible, or even particularly difficult, to get into college. (The years 2009–2010 are projected to be the last big class of kids applying to college. After that, the numbers go down significantly, meaning schools will have to strenuously compete for your child.) College is not something you or your child should obsess about. It is not Shangri-La. And *Princeton Review* notwithstanding, there are dozens if not hundreds of colleges where your child can get a great education and be happy. Sure, it is difficult to get into the most competitive top twenty or thirty schools, but there are many excellent colleges that are actively searching for students every single year, hoping to convince *your average kid* to come to their wonderful school.

However, we've pushed our kids so hard to perform in high school, they're bound to feel like failures if they don't get into the very most prestigious colleges. It's a vicious competitive circle. The overachievers I've talked to feel that all their

AP courses, SAT prep, travel soccer, service projects, and leadership awards have to add up to something big. And that something big is a high-status college that will announce to the world, *"I'm all that!"* If they end up at a college nobody's heard of, a college that anybody could get into, what was the point of all that work, all that striving, all that stress?

Good question. What *is* the point of kids killing themselves to achieve more, more, more in high school? Why do we act as if college is some huge marathon that you must prepare and train for, when everybody knows it's just a place to get away from your parents, do Jell-O shots, sleep with inappropriate people, and take bizarre and wonderful courses like "The History of Lesbians in Silent Film" and "Buddhist Social Ethics"? Why do we insist that every college applicant be a leader, or demonstrate "leadership qualities"? Leadership isn't a common commodity; it's actually quite rare. Where are all the good, essential followers going to come from?

As the parent of a junior, I admit I'm nervous about college applications, too. But I resent the hell out of that. I can neither completely buy into the hysteria nor rise above it, although for somebody as neurotic as me, it presents a virtually irresistible invitation to snap into panic mode. I routinely think I should be doing more to facilitate the process and get Lulu prepped and polished. Yet there is something about the engineered resumé of the typical affluent college applicant that kind of makes me sick. I can't help thinking: What happens to the kids whose parents can't afford the thousand-dollar tutoring to boost their SAT scores? The kids whose guidance counselors aren't shepherding them through the application process, setting up their test dates, and urging them to pad their resumés with feel-good community service projects and positions in clubs? What about the athletes who can't afford the sports camps, trainers, and travel leagues and have to scrape by on innate talent? Or the kids who won't have professional writers editing their personal essays and who may not even have a computer for the thirty-five obligatory rewrites?

This is not a level playing field; kids without resources aren't even in the same ballpark. And while I want my daughter to have all the advantages I can provide her, I have a lot of guilt about the millions of parents who lack those advantages. (That's also why I believe people who oppose affirmative action should have their heads—and hearts—examined.) The SAT and ACT tests are not "standardized" tests; they are inherently unfair. Unless everybody gets a tutor or nobody gets a tutor, they are deeply biased measures of intelligence and aptitude.

All this anxiety-ridden competition is focused on chasing the dream of getting into a Yale or Stanford, as if that is going to permanently ensure happiness. One of the *only* reasons I feel sorry for kids these days is this poisonous Ivy fixation. Parents need to seriously chill out and simply look for a college where their kid can get a good education and do well. Sure, the media tell you to get to work on your kid's college resumé *now*, while he's still in middle school. But it helps to ask yourself that favorite question among parents: *If all your friends jumped off a cliff, would you?* Before your values and common sense take a nosedive off the ledge in the stampede of mass hysteria over college admissions, take a breather. Opt out of the madness. Give your teen something greater to aspire to than an acceptance letter. Think beyond the next four years, which will no more make or break your kid's future than your college experience did yours. There's a whole big world out there.

Carpe diem.

WORDS OF WISDOM

My friend Joy lives in Santa Cruz, California, and she is the mother I dream of being if I were a totally different person. She's spent her life as an artist and spiritual seeker, and raised her two kids to think independently and follow their dreams. Her son, Micah, got a degree in film from UC San Diego and now works on the snowboard patrol in winters and for Outward Bound Australia in summers, while he writes screenplays. Her daughter, Arielle, decided not to go to college and is working in a coffee shop and art gallery to save up for a trip around the world. Joy is totally supportive of both their choices—even her daughter's choice (gulp!) not to go to college. In my heart, I know her kids will be creative, empowered, confident, and happy in their adventures and will become awesome adults. It makes me wonder why I'm so obsessed with Lulu's grades and myopic in my view of what's possible. I'm deeply envious of Joy's ability to go off the higher-ed grid, although I have to admit: That plays a lot better in California than on the career- and college-obsessed East Coast.

BOOMER AMNESIA

One of the most hilarious things about Boomer parents is our die-hard effort to erase our own pasts and prevent our children from doing the same things we did. So we tell little white lies along the lines of "I never inhaled" and "Well, I had a *few* relationships before I married your father" to try to bolster our shaky stance as pillars of morality. There's nothing terribly wrong with that. I've got a short list of things I've done that I would die if Lulu ever tried, too.

But along the same path of convenient forgetfulness, we have somehow also convinced ourselves (our own histories to the contrary) that life is a linear, rational progression from one thoughtful goal to the next. We act as if high school is the beginning of a long, narrow road to achievement, and that you can never veer off to become a surf bum or to waste a few years in a torrid, hopeless romance. We try earnestly to sell this success fantasy to our kids and convince them to climb aboard a career-planning train that we wouldn't have been caught dead on. Now, it might be quite possible for some people to map out their life when they are 17. But the vast majority of us had no idea what we were going to do when we entered—or exited—college, and if we had a plan, it was probably to delay reaching adulthood or making a career decision as long as possible. Remember the brilliant Talking Heads anthem—"Road to Nowhere"—that we used to play at brain-melting volume? I'm sure that song would be considered utterly subversive on the hyped-up career superhighway today's kids are on. My daughter as a junior routinely gets asked about her "career path" and what she wants to major in at college, and I'm afraid she is starting to feel weird that she has no earthly idea.

Truth is, the Road to Nowhere is exactly where a lot of kids should be before, during, and after college: out there exploring the world, putting on one job after another to see which fits best, and making their young adulthood a journey of discovery. That's certainly the way I found out what I wanted to do, and in today's constantly changing global marketplace, the ability to shift from one career to the next is probably the ultimate job security. Many jobs (if not careers) happen as a

Tales from Post Teens ● ● ● ● ● ● ● ● ●

I went to a pretty challenging college, so when I graduated, a lot of my friends went directly off to grad school. I had a degree in political science and psychology but I really didn't have any idea what I wanted to do as a career. I felt awful about that, like I was going to fall through some crack and never amount to anything. I even started to take the LSAT although I had no interest in law at all; I just wanted to feel like I had a plan. Right in the middle of my total panic attack, my mom's best friend took me on a weekend to the country and told me the whole story of how she graduated from college summa cum laude, but then had no idea what she was going to do and almost had a nervous breakdown. She's got a hugely successful career now and I never knew this story. She advised me to move anywhere in the country I'd always wanted to live, give myself a year to just waitress, get tan, and chill out, and only then start to think about what I might want to do. Of course I didn't exactly do that, because a job in my field opened up and I took it, but just having somebody say "Don't worry, relax, and the right thing will happen" took so much pressure off me. I'm sure my mom would have killed her friend if she knew she was telling me to go waitress in Hawaii with my $200,000 degree, but it really helped!

matter of serendipity, not five-year planning. You fall into something by talking to a friend's dad at a barbeque and find out it's what you were meant to do. Or it leads you circuitously to what you love.

If we Boomers can manage to put worry on hold for a minute, maybe we'll be able to reconnect with our own pasts and cut our kids a little slack when they go for their walka-bout. Have a little faith. They'll get where they need to go.

THEY STILL HEAR YOU

Teenagers like to pretend that you are merely flapping your lips to create a breeze, but the truth is, the words you say continue to enter their consciousness whether they want them to or not. And those words have an influence. So keep on giving your children messages you want them to hear about life, relationships, responsibility, how to live in the world, and how to be a good person. In other words, articulate the things you believe in, which hopefully you can still remember after five years of living with a disparaging teenager.

My sister Mary Lou likes to copy down funny, inspirational sayings and stick them on her refrigerator, above the kitchen table and on iridescent Post-it notes festooned around the house. A few recent ones were "Don't ask the Lord to guide your footsteps if you're not willing to move your feet" and "If opportunity doesn't knock, build a door." You can't help reading these little pep talks because they're right in front of you. Your eyes idly drift over the words—"Some succeed because they are destined to, but most suc-ceed because they are determined to"—and they sink right in. It's like subliminal advertising but without all the sex in the ice cubes.

Even if you're a teenager who thinks these messages are super-lame, your brain can't totally cancel them out because the sayings aren't critical or personal. The positive messaging is unblockable. My husband is anti-anything-stuck-on-any-thing (maybe it's a fear of flyers) but I love the idea and plan to implement it when his back is turned. What the heck: "If at first you don't succeed, try, try again."

My friend Michael has a similar tactic that helps him survive life with his four teenage daughters. He keeps a Gary Larson calendar on the kitchen counter and every day he starts the morning with a laugh, followed by the usual hysteria over missing soccer socks, bathroom hogging, and who called shotgun first. Before they launch into their brutal territorial battles, his girls all crowd around to read the cartoon together. It's the one good moment Michael can count on every day. (On the ineffective end of the spectrum: I bought a calendar of Shakespeare *bon mots* to share with Lulu and she never once looked at it and utterly resented my transparent attempt to refine her intellect.)

You can also employ the words your own parents beat into your head. My friend Monica Pearson, the first woman and first African American to anchor a news program in Atlanta, has mentored dozens of young women in their careers. Her speeches always feature a sampling of Hattie-isms, the adages she grew up hearing—and still hears—from her tiny, indefatigable 90-year-old mother. A small sampling include: "Anything worth having is worth working for." "It's what you do with what you have that makes you who you are." And my favorite (once you've taken the former advice and achieved great things) is this warning against pride: "Empty cans make the most noise."

Long after you're not around, the Mom-isms you repeat will reverberate in your kids' brains and influence them. I still remember my mother's and my grandmother's favorite sayings, even when I wish I didn't. So don't be afraid to be corny. Corn is one of the most ancient and basic nutrients in life (especially the candy form).

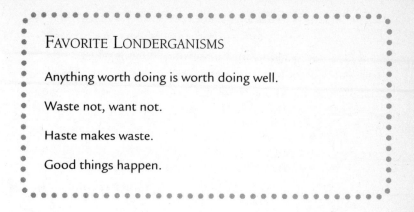

FAVORITE LONDERGANISMS

Anything worth doing is worth doing well.

Waste not, want not.

Haste makes waste.

Good things happen.

PRACTICE THIS MANTRA:
SUCKS TO BE YOU

With Acceptance comes the reality that you may have to sit by and watch your young adult do some profoundly dumb things. Without intervening to tell him *I told you so.* Or rushing in to save her. This is far more difficult than it sounds. (Of course, our parents were crystal-clear in how to cope with this stage: You were out of the house, on your own, and hell no, they weren't going to accept a collect call.) But we Boomer parents are so entwined with our kids, it can be difficult for us to differentiate between something that is happening to them and something that is happening to us. I've adopted one last fantastic saying from my favorite 20-something friends to help make those boundaries very clear and brilliantly convey: This is your problem, not mine.

Sucks to be you sounds a bit callous at first, but the inherent sarcasm can be softened with a dollop of compassion and empathy. *Sucks to be you* articulates the sadness of the universe when life turns against you and everything goes wrong. It's big enough to contain regret and resignation. It's small enough to be personal and trenchant. What it doesn't offer is an invitation to pull up a chair and unload all the problems that are causing one's life to suck. Or to express sentiments like "I'm right there in the trenches with you." It is laden with unspoken confidence that the fallen one can pick himself up and get back on track, but what is noticeably missing is any suggestion that the victim move back home so you can work it out together. Instead, it places the problem firmly in the other person's court.

Thus, when your son gets straight D's and then can't get into the program he wants, the appropriate parental response is: *Dang, sucks to be you.*

When your daughter gets caught making out with her boyfriend's best friend and is dumped by both guys, the appropriate parental response is: *Gee, sucks to be you.*

And when your young adult bounces a check to the IRS, the appropriate parental response is: *Wow, sucks to be you.*

Got it?

This mantra is not recommended for use when teens are still living under your roof and you truly are responsible for most of the things they do. Then it could be construed as a cold and heartless response (boo hoo). But once your teens achieve the Age of Reason (hilariously known as 18), have a go at it. You cannot believe how liberating it is.

15

THE PROMISED LAND

YOU WON'T DIE WITHOUT THEM.

This is hyperbole, of course. Logically, you know you'll probably live a lot longer without a teenager around to ratchet up your blood pressure into the stratosphere. But for some overinvested parents (*c'est moi!*) death by sadness at the loss of the teen's daily presence can feel like a distinct possibility.

However, with Acceptance comes the realization that you *can and will* survive separation from your teen. Sure, you'll miss all the life-threatening fun. The endless barrage of covert phone calls that end with you physically wrestling the cell phone from his hands at 2 A.M. The last-minute demand for mousse and deodorant that involves perilous high-speed trips to the Rite-Aid. The lurking boyfriend whom you have to chase off the roof. And of course, their need to stay out late and your need to wait up, which collide in a maelstrom of chronic sleep deprivation. Teens have to go away. Otherwise, the stress of trying to keep up with them is going to kill you.

Naturally, your life becomes a howling wilderness when they leave. You've managed to clear your calendar for the past eight years to attend your kids' games, show up at their concerts, volunteer at school, and drive them thousands of miles around the metropolitan area. Your current idea of a super-hot night probably involves a heating pad and an electric blanket. Clearly, you need to get out more. But it's going to take some time to work your way back into a real life.

First, you need to shed the habits of a day-to-day parent. What a bizarre transition! After eighteen years of centering your entire world on your children, you now have no place to put all that energy. Previously, your day was organized around your kids' schedule—the morning wakeup, breakfast, and rush to school; the afternoon lessons, after-school activities, and preparation for dinner; the nights filled with studying, papers, printer breakdowns, weekend social planning, laundry, athletics, and sleepovers. You gave your life to them wholeheartedly, and that was necessary and rewarding (for the most part). But now you need to reclaim your time.

Start with baby steps, like taking a morning yoga class or making a daily Starbucks pilgrimage. Go to art gallery openings after work, or meet friends for cocktails. Go out for brunch on the weekends. Read the whole paper; don't stop at the headlines. Catch the late show of a film (just don't pick anything with subtitles that you'll be tempted to snooze through). Park the car on Friday night and don't move it again until Sunday. Sleep in. Go out. Live it up.

You'll be okay. Seriously, it's great to have children but it's also great to have them grown. Remember, they're not gone. They will never be gone. They're just not living in the house anymore (which doesn't mean it's a good idea to tell them when you're going out of town, folks). Some things never change.

TALES FROM POST-TEENS • • • • • • • •

My mother and I fought constantly the whole time I was in high school. My older sister never fought with my mom and would tell her everything, as if they were best friends. I couldn't believe that—I was always telling her to stop it because I didn't want my mother to know anything about what I was doing and my chatty sister was making me look bad. I will say this as a positive, though. My mom and I stopped fighting once I went away to college and we became really close then. And my sister, who didn't talk back at all, was less close with her once she went away. Maybe I'm trying to justify myself here, but I think I fought with her because I knew I could and that she'd still love me. And once I got away, I felt like I could be close with her without her totally overwhelming me. Because I'm sort of in control of the relationship now, I find that I really want to talk to her and I actually let her in my life.

Space: The Final Frontier

Teenagers take up a lot of room, in every sense of the word. It's astonishing how one single child can fill up a house with emotions, problems, smells, sulks, joys, tears, dirty clothes, and laughter. Even when they're not speaking to you, their presence is there, sucking up all the oxygen in the house. So when your child goes off on his or her own, you're going to have a lot of space to fill.

This is an opportunity of immense proportions. You get to reinvent your life *and* your house! The first question is: When do you reclaim the kid's bedroom? Some parents keep the room a shrine for years; others rush in there and redecorate the first week of freshman year. It depends on how attached you are to your teen coming home, how attached your kid is to keeping his room intact, and how disgusted you are with the state of deterioration that's taken place over the course of the teen years. A general rule of thumb is that most kids will come home for the summer after freshman year of college and, the following summers, wing off to more exciting, permissive pastures. If it makes you feel better to keep her room preserved exactly as she left it, by all means do so. But if it helps to make the room into a tanning salon that obliterates all trace of him, go for it.

Beyond the physical space, eons of emotional and mental space are now available. For dads who have been building careers and cramming their craniums with sports statistics for years, this might not pose a severe problem. They can replace the grown child with Bolivian soccer or a new woodworking project. Moms, particularly those who don't work outside the home, are likely to experience the departure of the child with more grief and alarm. The hole ripped in their life acts like an open window in a plane, threatening to yank them out into a free fall. It's good to pack a parachute in preparation.

Try to have some projects in your back pocket to throw yourself into when your teenager moves out. Initially this might involve a new job, a volunteer opportunity that demands a lot of time and attention, or an extended spa vacation—anything that reintroduces you to the world at large. Over the long term, however, your new pursuit should be something that has real meaning for you, not merely takes up your time. What's going to be missing in your life is a sense of purpose and engagement; that is what you need to replace.

Personally, I think mothers who have survived the teen years make dream employees and should be the hottest commodity on *Monster.com*. These conflict-hardened gals don't know the meaning of a sick day. Surly bosses, backstabbing co-workers, and bitchy clients will seem like family. Experienced moms are brilliant multi-taskers, calm in a crisis, and could organize the invasion of Normandy in an afternoon, then toss in a couple dozen cupcakes for good measure. Statistics show that corporate America is sitting up and taking notice of their skills, and it's not only because they're consummate workhorses. It's because they're accomplished and ready to hit the ground running. So if taking on a new job appeals to you gals, go for it! (If you're uncertain over precisely where to focus your job search, by all means seek out the advice of a life coach or career counselor.)

The good news all around is that empty-nesters are not the moping, grief-stricken mourners you might expect. Research on the happiness of different age groups reveals that the one consistent characteristic of empty-nesters is a tendency to smile more. They're far more satisfied, content, and peaceful than parents of teenagers.

Why is this no surprise?

Join the parade.

REINVENTING YOUR LIFE

Of course, you can always go back to work. But in case that seems like a drastic measure that might eat up a lot of your time, here are a few other ventures to get you out of the house (critically important) and get you involved with people as frisky and fascinating as you. I call these "Invigorating Options for Parents of Post-Teens":

1. Adopt an elephant in Africa and spend a couple weeks at the David Sheldrick Trust Wildlife refuge, nursing 800-pound orphans back to health.

2. Volunteer for Habitat for Humanity and help build houses for less fortunate families. (Let a nail gun make your day!)
3. Take an Outward Bound course.
4. Join your church choir and torture unsuspecting parishioners with your singing voice.
5. Volunteer at your local public school to help kids with homework (unlike your teen, they'll let you!).
6. Plant a gazillion bulbs and new trees, join a gardening club, and discover the fantastic thrill of rototilling.
7. Take a cooking course in a cuisine your picky teen would never eat.
8. Visit every national and state park within a 100-mile radius.
9. Make a weekly visit to a retirement home or community center for seniors. They'll love it and you'll feel like a spring chicken.
10. Do that thing you always said you were going to when you had time—learn how to mosaic, play the drums, take up horseback riding, write a screenplay, become a docent, woodwork, paint, or go back to medical school.

Think big!

LET THE UNIVERSE HANDLE IT

Way back in the day, I went to a shrink and I remember spending an entire session complaining that life wasn't fair. I wanted somebody who had done me wrong to be punished, and I was deeply disappointed that justice wasn't forthcoming. My shrink, no doubt annoyed at all the bitching, said to me, "Why don't you just let the universe handle that?"

WORDS OF WISDOM

Bridget went back to work in nursing after spending twenty years at home raising her kids. She had to take some courses to learn the latest medical advances, procedures, and medications, and at first her hours were a bit crazy. But when people tried to commiserate with her about how difficult it must be to go back to work in such a challenging job, Bridget had to laugh. "When I was a young nurse, the hardest part of my job was when a doctor was impatient or unhappy with me, or a patient yelled at me about something. It used to tear me up. I'd literally go home in tears, I was so hurt and upset. But after raising three teenagers, nothing fazes me at all. I'm impervious to insults, stress, and people being mad at me. Compared to raising teenagers, this job is a piece of cake."

I was temporarily stunned into silence. What a concept! What if you could let go of everything you felt you had to personally oversee—righting injustice, meting out punishment for the wicked, finding out who isn't changing the toilet paper roll—and just let the universe handle it? Never mind the Bible passage that my mother used to love, "Why do you look at the speck that is in your brother's eye, but do not notice the log that is in your own eye?" We're talking self-righteous indignation here—and the absolute futility of it.

If you can allow the universe, karma, or divine retribution to settle scores for you, you'll be free to do more of the things you want, like starting your own recycling plant or finding a cure for crow's feet. It's amazing how much time you waste trying to figure out why the world doesn't work the way you think it should. Admittedly, I myself haven't fully grasped the concept yet, but I'm a lot more conscious of my own flaws, and that stupid log in my eye. Down the road, I predict I'll be keeping the universe super-busy with all the things I'm turning over.

Yet as life hands your adult child some real difficulties, you may feel an almost irresistible urge to intervene or retaliate on his or her behalf. "Let the universe handle it" is particularly potent when applied to parenting in this stage. Thus, when you long to hunt down and maim the jerk who broke your child's heart, turn it over to the universe instead. When your son gets passed over for that promotion he deserved, or somebody steals your daughter's great idea and rides it to the top, let the universe settle the score.

This philosophy is the opposite of intervention, which is why it feels so bizarre and foreign to me, *a.k.a.* Ms. Buttinsky. But I intuitively recognize its truth because, despite the difficulty involved in embracing it, it is the path to freedom— much like letting go of the child you raised and love more than life itself.

It's not up to you to decide how the universe rewards or punishes other people, any more than it's up to you to decide what happens in your child's life. You've done all you can, you've tried your best, and now you have to trust that things will work out okay. Or at least the way they're supposed to. If you look at your own life, you can clearly see that quite often the things you've resisted most strenuously, and resented most bitterly, have been the instruments of the greatest growth. Trying to circumvent uncomfortable forces of change and control outcome is not only futile, it is ultimately counterproductive. You can't protect your kids from life. Why would you want to?

Thanks to your good parenting, they can handle it. And so can the universe.

TALES FROM POST-TEENS • • • • • • • •

Whenever I complained or cried about something, my mom used to tell me, "Life isn't fair." She would simply state it as a fact—like we all should know that not everything is going to come out the way we think it should. She won with this tactic many, many times because I never could come up with a snappy comeback. Eventually I just became frustrated, recognized the truth in what she was saying, and ended my argument.

Many years later, when a friend was complaining about her job, I found myself using the same nonchalant "Life isn't fair" response. I laughed at the fact that my mother's words were literally coming out of my mouth, but I see now that her credo is a way to accept the flaws of life without really being angry with anyone. If you think about it, what we have been blessed with is way better than what would have been fair.

THE ROAD TO HAPPINESS

In case you're feeling truly blue, here's a technique that has been scientifically proven to increase happiness. (I am not making this up; the University of Pennsylvania has a couple geniuses devoted to the subject.) At the end of each day, think of three good things that happened and analyze why those things occurred. That's it.

For some of us, the technique sounds eerily similar to what our moms preached: Say your prayers every night and thank God for all your blessings. But even if you're an atheist, the exercise will be immediately rewarding, because you're focusing on good things happening, rather than on the long list of things you need to worry about and the people who've earned your wrath. By analyzing *why* those three things made you happy, you're focusing on your particular strengths: what fulfills and satisfies you. And that insight encourages you to seek out similar experiences.

Apparently we don't have a set point on our happiness index, as previously believed. It's true that life circumstances can increase or depress our happiness, but those variations are fairly temporary. The boost from getting married, for instance, lasts only about two years (duhhhhh). Having children, one of the great joys in life, takes a big toll on marital satisfaction and can lead to some severe life agony, as we know. (Parents actually gain in happiness as kids leave home.) Apparently, too, most of the things that we think will make us happy don't. Income doesn't have much effect (above the poverty level). Sex? Not really. Health? Sure, but not as much as you might suspect.

It seems that people who feel productive, are positive, and appreciate things in their lives are happy. Focus on that.

Three good things are all it takes.

THEY NEVER REALLY LEAVE

Did you ever break up with a lover and think you'd die if you didn't get him back, then you did and wondered why in God's name you thought you couldn't live without him? You may experience a bit of that same emotion when the children you miss acutely finally come home. Day 1 is bliss. Day 2 is okay, with a few noticeable fissures as unpleasant habits resurface. On Day 3, all hell breaks loose and you can't wait for them to go away again and leave you in peace.

Unlike your past horrible relationships, however, there will probably never come a time when you don't long to see and be with your kids. No matter how agonizing the teenage years, you'll always love those children of yours and want them (temporarily) around. Once teens are freed from your tyrannical reign and can go off and create the lives they desire, they may even return to a semblance of the happy people they were as toddlers. As they lose that perpetual scowl and regain control of their sassy mouths, you're likely to fall in love with them all over again. Grown-up kids are interested in what you have to say. They want to tell you what's going on in their lives. They may even believe you have something to offer them beyond tuition and health insurance. As the old saying goes, "I can't believe how much my parents learned between the time I was 18 and 25."

Thomas Wolfe was right: You can't go home again. But you can never quite leave, either. You and your children are bound together for life, and astonishingly, considering how exhausting it was to get through the past six years, you still hopefully have decades of time in front of you. Time to watch them develop a career. Fall in love. Have kids of their own. And become the unique and incredible individuals you knew were within.

Acceptance means that you can let them go, knowing they will be okay. Not perfect, but okay. It's being thankful that your prayers of surviving your teens' adolescence have been answered, even if God obviously wasn't paying attention to the full litany of your requests. And it means not dwelling on all the things you didn't do and all the times you screwed up, but giving yourself an A for effort and a B- for execution.

It isn't over. Family is never over; that's the beauty and claustrophobia of it. You'll always have each other to cling to, flail against, and, most important, to forgive.

That's what agony, I mean *love*, is.

Amen.

ACKNOWLEDGMENTS

I like to say this book practically wrote itself, but in fact, that's a whopping lie.

Obviously, I am swimming in gratitude for the hundreds of stories that friends and family shared with me from their own teenaged years and their own parenting trials. Liz Meitus, Abbie Galardi, Donna Milligan, Sarah Tomley, Staci Katz, Amy Laurenza & posse, Karen Kahldahl, Jimmy Ebersole, Laurie Dibeler, Cheryl Dixon, Ginger O'Neill, Jean O'Neill, Joy Diamond, Dana Kleiman, Anne Frankenfield, Judith Hain, Fred Augustern, Kate Martin, Dick Graglia, Rita Marshall, Chris Purse, Nancy Rebek, Clarice Bonzer, Mimi Kaupe, Michelle Botelho, TimDickSusanKathyMaryLou-BonnieTommy Londergan, and the dozens of folks whose names have been changed to protect the guilty—thanks for your breathtaking honesty and brilliant candor.

Thanks to my agent, Daniel Lazar, for his tireless support of the concept and for being such a receptive, hilarious enabler.

Thanks also to Amy Berkower for her original enthusiasm that made me believe it was a good idea to capture the agony.

A special shout-out to my patient and inspired editor, Katie McHugh; my fastidious and grammatically gifted copy editor, Christine Arden; and my editorial coordinator extraordinaire, Cisca Schreefel. It blows my mind all the work you have done to make my little book come to life.

Finally, I'd like to thank my own parents, Tom and Dorothy Mae, for getting me through my own agonizing teenage years, and Jaime, Lindsay, Lulu, and Tyler for giving me the immense privilege of sharing your adolescence, watching you become the amazing people you've turned into, and allowing me to shamelessly exploit the experience. A final word of praise for my beloved husband Larry who encourages me to write books when I could be doing something a lot more profitable, and even after twelve years of marriage still thinks I'm funny.

I love you guys!

INDEX

Page numbers in italics indicate boxed text.